S0-BYN-032

Barnard College

New York, New York

Written by Megan Cloud
Edited by Carolyn Keller

Additional contributions by Christina Koshzow, Chris Mason, Omid Gohari, Joey Rahimi, Luke Skurman, Allison Drash, Tim Williams, Adam Burns, Jon Skindzier and Kristen Burns

ISBN # 1-59658-007-0
ISSN # 1551-9481
© Copyright 2005 College Prowler
All Rights Reserved
Printed in the U.S.A.
www.collegeprowler.com

Special thanks to Babs Carryer, Andy Hannah, LaunchCyte, Tim O'Brien, Bob Sehlinger, Thomas Emerson, Andrew Skurman, Barbara Skurman, Bert Mann, Dave Lehman, Daniel Fayock, Chris Babyak, The Donald H. Jones Center for Entrepreneurship, Terry Slease, Jerry McGinnis, Bill Ecenberger, Idie McGinty, Kyle Russell, Jacque Zaremba, Larry Winderbaum, Paul Kelly, Roland Allen, Jon Reider, Team Evankovich, Julie Fenstermaker, Lauren Varacalli, Abu Noaman, Jason Putorti, Mark Exler, Daniel Steinmeyer, Jared Cohon, Gabriela Oates, Tri Ad Litho, David Koegler, Glen Meakem.

Bounce Back Team: Katie Sosnuck and Roxana Azizi

College Prowler™
5001 Baum Blvd.
Suite 456
Pittsburgh, PA 15213

Phone: (412) 697-1390, 1(800) 290-2682
Fax: (412) 697-1396, 1(800) 772-4972
E-mail: info@collegeprowler.com
Website: www.collegeprowler.com

College Prowler™ is not sponsored by, affiliated with, or approved by Barnard College in any way.

College Prowler™ strives faithfully to record its sources. As the reader understands, opinions, impressions, and experiences are necessarily personal and unique. Accordingly, there are, and can be, no guarantees of future satisfaction extended to the reader.

© Copyright 2005 College Prowler. All rights reserved. No part of this work may be reproduced or transmitted in any form or by any means, including but not limited to, photocopy, recording, or any information storage and retrieval systems, without the express written permission of College Prowler™.

Welcome to College Prowler™

During the writing of College Prowler's guidebooks, we felt it was critical that our content was unbiased and unaffiliated with any college or university. We think it's important that our readers get honest information and a realistic impression of the student opinions on any campus — that's why if any aspect of a particular school is terrible, we (unlike a campus brochure) intend to publish it. While we do keep an eye out for the occasional extremist — the cheerleader or the cynic — we take pride in letting the students tell it like it is. We strive to create a book that's as representative as possible of each particular campus. Our books cover both the good and the bad, and whether the survey responses point to recurring trends or a variation in opinion, these sentiments are directly and proportionally expressed through our guides.

College Prowler guidebooks are in the hands of students throughout the entire process of their creation. Because you can't make student-written guides without the students, we have students at each campus who help write, randomly survey their peers, edit, layout, and perform accuracy checks on every book that we publish. From the very beginning, student writers gather the most up-to-date stats, facts, and inside information on their colleges. They fill each section with student quotes and summarize the findings in editorial reviews. In addition, each school receives a collection of letter grades (A through F) that reflect student opinion and help to represent contentment, prominence, or satisfaction for each of our 20 specific categories. Just as in grade school, the higher the mark the more content, more prominent, or more satisfied the students are with the particular category.

Once a book is written, additional students serve as editors and check for accuracy even more extensively. Our bounce-back team — a group of randomly selected students who have no involvement with the project — are asked to read over the material in order to help ensure that the book accurately expresses every aspect of the university and its students. This same process is applied to the 200-plus schools College Prowler currently covers. Each book is the result of endless student contributions, hundreds of pages of research and writing, and countless hours of hard work. All of this has led to the creation of a student information network that stretches across the nation to every school that we cover. It's no easy accomplishment, but it's the reason that our guides are such a great resource.

When reading our books and looking at our grades, keep in mind that every college is different and that the students who make up each school are not uniform — as a result, it is important to assess schools on a case-by-case basis. Because it's impossible to summarize an entire school with a single number or description, each book provides a dialogue, not a decision, that's made up of 20 different topics and hundreds of student quotes. In the end, we hope that this guide will serve as a valuable tool in your college selection process. Enjoy!

OMID GOHARI ◯ CHRISTINA KOSHZOW ◯ CHRIS MASON ◯ JOEY RAHIMI ◯ LUKE SKURMAN ◯
The College Prowler™ Team

Table of Contents

Introduction from the Author

"Why would you want to go to an all-girls school?" and "where is that?" These were questions I got all the time when I selected Barnard College as my college of choice. Although it is very well known and respected in New York and other places, Barnard is usually not known at all in a good part of the country. Its reputation is growing, though. Early admission and regular admission applications to the college have been steadily growing in the past few years, while the acceptance rate has been declining. This is mostly the result of a young and vibrant college administration, many of whom are Barnard Alumnae themselves.

Barnard College holds a strange and unique place among colleges today. It's a women's college and part of the Seven Sisters left from an era in which very few women could get a college education at all. Yet, Barnard exists now in day in which a woman going for her bachelor's degree is sometimes a foregone conclusion, giving women the opportunity to choose to go to a single-sex college rather than it being the only option. Barnard is also part of world-renowned Columbia University, giving Barnard's students access to more academic options and the all important 'Y' chromosome. Many people focus on this affiliation unnecessarily because of the prestigious Columbia name, however there are many classes that BC students would never take anywhere else and are very proud of, like those in the dance and architecture programs. In fact, many Columbia College students elect to take writing classes, among others, because of the one-on-one attention that Barnard's small classes afford.

The truth of the matter is that for most women graduating from high school, the choice to attend an all-girls school can be a difficult one to make, especially if that is not an environment that you're used to. I would urge anyone interested in the school to read on to discover that, while enrolling only girls is a very obvious Barnard trait, for better or for worse, it certainly isn't the only notable one.

Megan Cloud, Author
Barnard College

By the Numbers

General Information

Barnard College
3009 Broadway
New York, New York 10027

Control:
Private; affiliated with
Columbia University

Academic Calendar:
Semester

Religious Affiliation:
None

Founded:
1889

Website:
http://www.barnard.edu

Main Phone:
(212) 854-5262

Admissions Phone:
(212) 854-2014

Student Body

**Full-Time
Undergraduates:**
2,232

**Part-Time
Undergraduates:**
49

**Full-Time Male
Undergraduates:**
0

**Full-Time Female
Undergraduates:**
2,232

Admissions

Overall Acceptance Rate:
27%

Regular Acceptance Rate:
30%

Early Decision Acceptance Rate:
41%

Total Applicants:
4,380

Total Acceptances:
1,201

Freshman Enrollment:
560

Yield (% of admitted students who actually enroll):
47%

Early Decision Available?
Yes

Early Action Available?
No

Total Early Decision Applicants:
405

Total Early Decision Acceptances:
167

Early Decision Deadline:
November 15

Early Decision Notification:
December 15

Regular Decision Deadline:
January 1

Regular Decision Notification:
Early April

Must-Reply-By Date:
May 1

Common Application Accepted?
No

Admissions Phone:
(212) 854-2014

Admissions E-mail:
admissions@barnard.edu

Admissions Website:
http://www.barnard.edu/admiss/

SAT I or ACT Required?
Yes, Either

First-Year Students Submitting SAT Scores:
90%

SAT I Range (25th – 75th Percentile):
1250-1410

SAT I Verbal Range (25th – 75th Percentile):
650-730

SAT I Math Range (25th – 75th Percentile):
630-700

Retention Rate:
94%

SAT II Requirements for Barnard College:

Writing or Literature, plus any two others if you are submitting SAT I scores

Top 10% of High School Class:
82%

Application Fee:
$45

Qualified applicants placed on waiting list:
766

Applicants accepting a place on waiting list:
507

Students enrolled from waiting list:
36

Transfer applications received for Fall 2003:
375

Transfer applicants offered admission for Fall 2003:
128

Transfer applicants enrolled for Fall 2003:
81

Financial Information

Full-Time Tuition:
$28,340

Room and Board:
$10,596

Books and Supplies for class:
$1,000 (average for the year)

Average Need-Based Financial Aid Package:
$25,424
(including loans, work-study, grants, and other sources)

Students Who Applied For Financial Aid:
55%

Students Who Received Aid:
80%

Students Who Applied For Financial Aid and Received It:
42%

Financial Aid Forms Deadline:
Regular Decision—February 1;
Early Decision—November 15

Financial Aid Phone:
(212) 854-2154

Financial Aid E-mail:
finaid@barnard.edu

Financial Aid Website:
http://www.barnard.edu/
services/fa.html

Academics

The Lowdown On...
Academics

Degrees Awarded:
Bachelor's

Most Popular Areas of Study:
Social Sciences
English
Performing Arts
Biological Sciences

Full-Time Faculty:
185

Faculty with Terminal Degree:
88%

Student-to-Faculty Ratio: 10:1

Popular Majors
13% psychology
12% English and literature
12% economics
9% political science and government
7% history

Average Course Load:
5

Special Degree Options

Five-year A.B. degree from Barnard and M.L.A. from Columbia's School of International and Public Affairs; five-year Barnard A.B. and M.P.A. from Columbia's Graduate Program in Public Policy and Administration; five-year Barnard A.B. and B.S. from Columbia's Fu Foundation School of Engineering and Applied Science. Qualified students may be nominated to enter Columbia Law School after three years at Barnard. Qualified students may enter Columbia's School of Oral and Dental Surgery after three years at Barnard; Barnard A.B. and another undergraduate degree from the Jewish Theological Seminary; Music students may qualify for a Barnard A.B. and a Master of Music from Juilliard

Graduation Rate

Four-year graduation rate: 75%

Five-year graduation rate: 84%

Average six-year graduation rate: 84%

AP Test Score Requirements

Possible credit for scores of 4 or 5

Did You Know?

• Barnard's number of female professors is **twice** the national average.

• At Barnard you'll want to check out **how many points** each class you take is worth. Points are similar to "hours" at other colleges, but they don't always exactly equal the amount of time you spend in class per week.

Sample Academic Clubs:

Biology Club, Neuroscience Journal Club, Psychology Club

Best Places to Study

The Lawn, Upper Level Mac

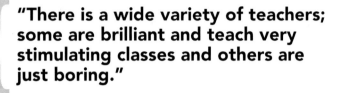

"There is a wide variety of teachers; some are brilliant and teach very stimulating classes and others are just boring."

Q "For the most part, **teachers are very approachable** and make their classes really interesting."

Q "I have had some really great teachers and some horrible teachers during my time at Barnard. **It all depends on the department**. Overall, however, they are all very approachable and really try to help students out. There are, of course, the few who don't care and can't teach the material effectively. The majority of the teachers here are pretty good at teaching the material and really aren't intimidating at all."

Q "Classes at Barnard are smaller than many of the courses at Columbia, and **generally the professor knows everybody's name**. They make themselves easily accessible and they encourage students to drop by their office hours, send them an e-mail, and most importantly, to not be afraid to ask questions."

Q "Like most schools, **you have teachers who are not so good and teachers who are amazing**. CULPA is usually accurate and I always use it when I register for classes."

Q "They have been pretty good and always try to help for the most part, though **a few have been a bit spacey**."

Q "While Barnard professors are often keeping themselves busy with teaching, grading papers and responding to their students' needs and concerns, they still somehow manage to contribute their knowledge and insight to the academic world. **They are authors, researchers, translators, poets, scientists and artists.** I've rarely encountered a professor who did not possess talent, intelligence and a genuine passion for his or her area of expertise. Here and there you may find a professor who is not exactly to your liking, but it is hard to not see some virtue in the professor's contributions."

Q "It's not every day that you can find a teacher who will invite the class over for coffee or take you out for lunch to discuss a paper, but at Barnard, this is not an uncommon occurrence. **Some of the greatest teachers I've ever had have been at Barnard**, not only because they are very fluent in their fields, but also because they are here because they love teaching. The same cannot always be said across the street at Columbia College, a place where research and book publishing may often take precedence over teaching."

Q "The teachers are pretty accepting most of the time and usually **seem interested in what they teach**, although that doesn't necessarily mean they're good at teaching. They are also usually available outside of class and welcome questions."

Q "Generally, I've had really good experiences with my professors. They're really accommodating, very willing to answer questions, make suggestions, etc. **Every professor I've had has been extremely passionate about the subject** he or she is teaching, which is always a positive thing. Their intelligence can, at times, be intimidating, and you do occasionally run into a professor who just doesn't work for you, but that holds true for all schools."

Q "I would say the caliber is excellent and superior to most universities, based on my experience as a transfer. However, they are busy people and, as **all professors seem to be, concerned with publishing and their own research.** They demand that you be organized and efficient in dealing with them. Also, teachers at Barnard tend to nurture more, since they are accustomed to dealing with complicated women."

Q "All the professors I've had were **friendly and available** for outside help."

The College Prowler Take On...
Academics

The teachers at Barnard are really some of the college's best assets. You will find that in contrast to other schools, the teaching assistants (TAs) only grade papers, proctor exams and offer additional help on homework. This is not only true for introductory lectures, but for labs and recitations as well. For the most part, teachers at Barnard are very accessible, and will accommodate students who need extra help. Professors have been known to even give out their home phone number, if the need arises. Of course, this isn't to say that there is no variation among the teaching staff, only that the odds of getting a professor who will make time to learn your name and answer specific questions are very good. One of the major things that a prospective student should be aware of when looking into Barnard is that classes are open for cross-registration throughout Columbia University's undergraduate colleges, which means that courses may be taken at the Fu Foundation School of Engineering and Applied Science (SEAS), Columbia College and Barnard College. This means Barnard professors are tenured by both Barnard College and Columbia University. However, it also means you might, and almost certainly will, take a class at Columbia. The only bad thing about Barnard's affiliation with Columbia is that graduate student TAs teach all lab sections and popular courses, like Calculus IA. TAs aren't all bad. They are just less concerned with student welfare in their course than a full professor might be. The best way to find out about a professor or a TA at any of the colleges is to look at the website, http://culpa.info, which is a site that allows students to give reviews on a professor's teaching style and workload.

B+

The College Prowler™ Grade on
Academics: B+

A high Academics grade generally indicates that professors are knowledgeable, accessible, and genuinely interested in their students' welfare. Other determining factors include class size, how well professors communicate, and whether or not classes are engaging.

Local Atmosphere

The Lowdown On...
Local Atmosphere

Region:
Northeast

City, State:
New York, New York

Setting:
Urban

Distance from Boston:
3.5 hours

Distance from Philadelphia:
2 hours

Points of Interest:
Cathedral of St. John the Divine (112th & Amsterdam)
Grant's Tomb (122nd & Riverside)
The Empire State Building
Grand Central Station,
Museum of Natural History
Metropolitan Museum of Art
Modern Art Museum
Central Park

➡

Closest Movie Theatres:

Loews Cineplex Harlem
2309 Frederick Douglass
Blvd, Harlem

Clearview Metro Twin
2626 Broadway, Upper West
Side

Loews Cineplex 84th Street Theatre
2310 Broadway, Upper West
Side

Loews Cineplex Lincoln Square
1998 Broadway, Upper West
Side

Closest Shopping Malls:

The Shops at Columbus Circle
10 Columbus Circle, Upper
West Side

Major Sports Teams:

New York Jets

New York Rangers

New York Yankees

New York Mets

City Websites
http://www.nyc.gov

Local Slang:

The City- how people refer to Manhattan.

Downtown- any place south of your current location in
Manhattan or referring to places south of Midtown

Uptown- any place north of your current location in
Manhattan or places north of Midtown

Did You Know?

5 Fun Facts about New York:

1. Central Park, the biggest in the city, is **843 acres.**

2. Broadway began as an **Algonquin trade route** called the Wiechquaekeck Trail.

3. John Hertz, who founded the **Yellow Cab Company** in 1907, chose yellow because he had read a study conducted by the University of Chicago that indicated it was the easiest color to spot.

4. Babe Ruth hit the **first home run** in Yankee Stadium in the first game ever played there.

5. The world's **largest gothic cathedral** is the Cathedral Church of St. John the Divine, and it's still under construction. Its first stone was laid in 1892.

Famous People from New York:

John Jay, jurist

Vince Lombardi, football coach

Washington Irving, author

Sean Combs, musician

Christopher Reeve, actor

Norman Rockwell, painter

Barbra Streisand, singer-actress

Claire Danes, actress

Students Speak Out On...
Local Atmosphere

> "I love the city atmosphere. There's so much to do, no matter what you like, and there are several universities nearby. You just have to be careful walking around really late if you're by yourself."

Q "New York City is a very fast paced environment. Since Barnard is located right next to Columbia and NYU is only a subway ride away, **there are too many places to go** and very few to avoid. It makes doing work hard."

Q "New York is a great place to live with so many resources and an endless amount of things to do. However, if not taking advantage of the arts and cultural opportunities that NYC has to offer, **I stay within the confines of Morningside Heights**. With the other three undergraduate schools at Columbia University—Columbia College, the School of Engineering and Applied Sciences (a.k.a. SEAS), and the School of General Studies (a.k.a. GS)—there are plenty of undergraduates to populate this part of town and provide some excitement."

Q "Very few colleges can offer a small campus community under the guise of a large university in a big city. Essentially, that is what sums up the atmosphere at Barnard. Barnard is a small, independent liberal arts school. **We have our own little campus,** complete with library, dorms, classrooms and a grassy knoll where students sit and read, suntan or play Frisbee."

Q **"The entire neighborhood is known for its college-town feel,** and it's also home to the Jewish Theological Seminary, the Union Theological Seminary, the Manhattan School of Music, and the Bank Street College of Education in addition to Columbia's numerous graduate and undergraduate schools. The neighborhood is filled with student-friendly bars, restaurants, independent gift shops and bookstores."

Q **"The area attracts a lot of families,** not only because the Columbia area is well known for its safety, but also because of its proximity to Riverside Park where students can go running, parents can play ball with their children, and film or photography students can find their inspiration."

Q "New York is the best place to go to school. It's full of really incredible opportunities and experiences. **Some of the best theater, shopping and dining in the world are only a subway ride away.** The university offers some really great deals, and a lot of classes on campus take advantage of the fabulous cityscape by arranging field trips to the Met, Central Park or the theater. It can get kind of expensive, but if you know where to look, you can save a lot of money."

Q "**New York City has lots to offer.** There are many other universities in the area. I don't think there is anything specifically to stay away from that there wouldn't be other schools. There are many places to visits, tourist sites, museums, and clubs."

Q "There are many schools in the New York City area, it's very busy, and **there are always places to visit or things to do**. On the other hand, urban areas, especially up near Harlem, can get dangerous and people should use caution."

"**The atmosphere is great!** Barnard is in the middle of New York City while not exactly in mid-town Manhattan. Easy access to anything—restaurants, clubs, stores—while still maintaining a private campus area."

"New York is amazing! Go downtown ,Chinatown, Little Italy, Greenwich, etc. **Go to the museums** and all the touristy stuff."

The College Prowler Take On...
Local Atmosphere

According to Barnard students, there's something for everyone in this city, but in a city as big as NYC you might have to search a little bit. New York City and the neighborhood of Morningside Heights really provides the best of both worlds for Barnard students, because while there is world class entertainment, dining and cultural events going on all the time all over the city; there is also a very small neighborhood, college town feel to Morningside Heights. In the area surrounding Barnard, you can wander into shops or cafés and expect to see someone you know, which really fosters a sense of community that a person might be surprised to find in New York City. There is something for everyone around the Barnard campus. Due to the close proximity of all these different groups of people, there is an energy that comes from the city that a person might not find in many other places while still being able to enjoy the familiarity of a small neighborhood. Of course, there are many other colleges around, such as Columbia College, the School of Engineering and Applied Sciences, Manhattan School of Music and the Jewish Theological Seminary. Morningside Heights is pretty much a neighborhood of just college students and professors that live nearby. Because there is nothing you can't find in the city, from Broadway to basketball to simple peace and quiet, Barnard is really located in a great city, and as New York asserts, "The Greatest City in the World".

The College Prowler™ Grade on
Local Atmosphere: A-

A high Local Atmosphere grade indicates that the area surrounding campus is safe and scenic. Other factors include nearby attractions, proximity to other schools, and the town's attitude toward students

Safety & Security

The Lowdown On...
Safety & Security

Number of Barnard Police: 25-30

Safety Services:
Blue light emergency call boxes
University Shuttle Bus
Barnard Escort Service
Columbia/Barnard Rape Crisis/Anti-Violence Support

Public Safety Phone:

(212) 854-3362

Health Services:
Basic Medical services
on-site pharmaceuticals
STD and Pregnancy screening
contraceptives
abortion services
counseling services

Health Center Office Hours

Monday through Friday from 8:30 a.m. to 5 p.m.

Did You Know?

• Students who present **college IDs** may ride on a University shuttle bus stopping between 108th and 125th Streets. The bus runs from 7 p.m. to 2:30 a.m. and picks up right outside Columbia's gates.

Students Speak Out On...
Safety & Security

{ **"Security and safety are very hard to achieve in New York City, but I think they do the best that they can."**

Q "**Security is pretty good.** There's a booth on every corner and they are even available to escort us at night if we don't feel safe."

Q "**I've never felt like I was in dange**r, but at the same time, the security system is very lax."

Q "Security is pretty good. **There are guards all over campus all the time**. There is also an escort service that will take students from one part of the campus to another and even from Barnard to Columbia."

Q "I've never heard of anything happening on campus, so I assume **security must be tight.**"

Q "I haven't had enough personal experience with either to really make an educated statement, but I usually feel pretty secure on campus. **One of the nice things about Barnard is the safe-ride system**. If it's late, and you need to get from one Barnard dorm to another, you can call a car from the security office to pick you up and drive you."

Q "**Barnard really takes care of their girls**. We have twenty-four-hour security booths on each corner all around campus and along the way towards the dorms. There are twenty-four hour desk attendants in every resident hall as well as the security resources provided by Columbia."

Q "Security is just fine. If you're walking home and it's dark, it makes you feel better to know that **a security guard is within yelling distance**."

The College Prowler Take On...
Safety & Security

Most students have never had specific dealings with the campus security, but they all know where to go should they ever need them. Barnard's security is very visible, which probably one of the greatest reasons that there's so little crime in the area, at least as it pertains to Barnard students on campus. There are security guards at every entrance into Barnard and at three other booths along side streets where Barnard dorms are located. There are also desk attendants in all of the dorms who must check for Barnard/Columbia ID before they allow you to enter the building, or if you have a visitor, the desk attendant must sign them in and keep their ID until they leave.

Aside from the visibility of Barnard security, they also provide an escort service that will drive students between dorms, or to different ends of campus if they ever feel unsafe walking around campus late at night. Most students haven't even used this service, but it's always comforting to know that it's there. Most people know when they come to Barnard that the campus isn't located in the best part of town, but once school starts very few feel concerned about their safety while on campus.

The only place that security loses points is that their role on campus is not clearly defined. Many students are not sure what is the responsibility of campus security and what is the responsibility of city police. While the security officers are able to escort suspicious people off of campus, they have no authority to detain anyone as the police can. They also aren't able to do anything legally if something is stolen. Again, Barnard security is very good at creating a safe feeling atmosphere for students to live and study in, but beyond that they really don't do much more.

B

The College Prowler™ Grade on

Safety &
Security: B

A high grade in Safety & Security means that students generally feel safe, campus police are visible, blue-light phones and escort services are readily available, and safety precautions are not overly necessary.

Computers

The Lowdown On...
Computers

High-Speed Network?
Yes.

Wireless Network?
Yes, in selected places

Number of Labs:
7

Numbers of Computers:
Around 150

Operating Systems:
PC, MAC, UNIX

Free Software

None

Discounted Software:

Windows, Mac OS X

24-Hour Labs

Brooks, Sulzberger, Plimpton, and 616

Charge to Print?

No, unless your printing needs are above a hundred pages a week.

Did You Know?

• Are you good with computers? You can sign up to help other Barnard students keep theirs up and running by being an **RCA.** Like RAs, RCAs also get certain perks for their service to the Barnard Community.

• Just need to check your email between classes? There are a few computers in upper level Mac to surf on for a few minutes **between classes.**

Students Speak Out On...
Computers

{ **"Bring your own computer if you can. If not, there are always places to work. You may just have to search a bit."**

Q "Computer labs are pretty crowded during finals and during certain times during the day, like lunch time. **I would say definitely bring your own computer**, but if you can't, then you can rely on always finding a computer anywhere on the Barnard or Columbia campus."

Q "The computer labs are usually half full except for around peak times. **The computer network is also good.** I'm rarely kicked offline."

Q "The computer labs located in the basement of dormitories are often very packed, but one always has the option of going to **use the lab in the Barnard library.**"

Q "Having your own computer is always helpful especially since **we have high speed Ethernet in every dorm** and suite. However, the computer labs are useful especially when you have a lot to print—given you have free printing within the allotted quota."

Q "**The computer lab in the library is usually pretty crowded**, so bringing your own computer is probably the best way to go."

Q "The computer labs are very busy and **it's hard to get a computer,** especially during midterms and finals. You should definitely bring your own computer."

Q "Most Barnard students will tell you that it's best to bring your own computer and your own printer. Although **both the library and most dormitories are equipped with computers and printers**, they can often be crowded and the college recently instated a hundred pages per week limit. While the quota can be useful in preventing students from printing unnecessary material from the internet or 300 fliers for the student government's upcoming bake sale, the quota can also make it very hard for a student who does not have her own printer."

Q "**The labs in the dorms are especially poorly maintained**. The computers are not shut down each day and even though they are fairly new Dell computers, they run slowly because they are always in use and there is no one to run Norton and Adware every few weeks. There is never anyone on site at the computer labs in the dorms to help you if a computer stops working properly. When it gets late and you need to print out that last-minute essay, you are often out of luck if the printer becomes jammed, runs out of paper or the ink cartridge needs to be replaced. During business hours there is a number you can call for help if something goes wrong, but for the most part, you're on your own."

Q "The library labs are your best bet, because they usually have people on staff to help you with technical issues. For this reason, they are also the most crowded and you may have to wait in line to get a computer. **The college primarily offers PCs to students,** although there are several Macintosh computers in the library and about one Mac computer per lab in each dorm. If you are a film concentrate or you work doing graphic design, the Barnard Media Center has about two or three Mac computers with Final Cut Pro 4.0 and Photoshop, among other programs."

Q "Having your own **computer is a plus**, but if you need one, they aren't impossible to come by."

The College Prowler Take On...
Computers

Personal computers at Barnard are close to essential. Yes, there are plenty of computer labs and printers, but due the volume of students using them, not just Barnard students, but all Columbia University students, they tend to be crowded and often times not working. Another hassle is the NINJa printing system, which limits students to a hundred pages of printing per week in the computer labs. To Barnard's credit, nothing in the computer labs stays broken very long, but it is a very common occurrence for printers to be out of commission. On the plus side, the network provided for students is very fast and reliable. There are enough internet connections to accommodate two people in most rooms, and there are also internet connections in the labs for people who bring their laptops.

Having said that, it is possible for a student to get along without her own personal computer. Really, if you have the patience of a saint, and don't mind hanging around the computer lab, then go for it. However, if the idea of sitting around watching some girl play solitaire when you need to write a paper makes you want to scream, you should probably look into purchasing your own computer. The case at Barnard is that most people have their own computer and use the computer labs mostly to check email and do work between classes or simply to print. While it is suggested that students bring their own computer, those that do not won't suffer here.

B-

The College Prowler™ Grade on

Computers: B-

A high grade in Computers designates that computer labs are available, the computer network is easily accessible, and the campus' computing technology is up-to-date.

Facilities

The Lowdown On...
Facilities

Student Center:
McIntosh Student Center

Campus size: 4 acres

Athletic Center:
LeFrak Gymnasium
Dodge Fitness Center

Libraries:
1

Popular Places to Chill:
The lawn
McIntosh Student Center

Housing Stats:
coed dorms (6%), women's dorms (60%), apartment for single students (34%), special housing for disabled students

What Is There to Do On Campus?

Between classes, you can see a play in the Minor Latham Playhouse or watch a movie in upper level Mac.

Movie Theatre on Campus?

No, but movies are often shown in various locations around campus, usually because a club has sponsored it.

Bar on Campus?

No

Bowling on Campus?

No

Coffeehouse on Campus?

Yes, Java City, located in upper level McIntosh

Favorite Things to Do:

Grab some coffee at Java City, read on the lawn, and rest for a while or talk with friends on the couches in upper level Mac.

Students Speak Out On...
Facilities

> "The athletic facilities could be better, as well as the student center, but basically we are connected to Columbia's facilities so it really doesn't matter."

Q "Since Barnard shares facilities with Columbia, most facilities are at Columbia. Since Columbia has a large student body, it has to have at least decent facilities. **They have great athletic facilities,** including the best fitness center I've ever seen, lots of computers, etc. Barnard has great student facilities, such as a counseling center to help students with any problems they might be having in classes or out of class."

Q "I have no basis for judgment on athletics, but there are many computer labs, in academic buildings as well as dorms. **Both Barnard and Columbia libraries are great resources.**"

Q "Barnard's gym is very small and has weird hours, but that has never been a problem since **all BC students have access to Columbia's Dodge Fitness Center**. Most people work out there. Our student center is quaint and by no means 'state of the art,' but it does the job nicely."

Q "We have many things available to us. There's a small weight room available for us as well as many computer labs. **We have nice things but nothing out of the ordinary.**"

Q "Columbia's facilities are much better, but they also have more students. However, **I do like McIntosh a lot.**"

Q "The really nice thing about Barnard is the fact that you have access to a really wide assortment of facilities. Columbia has a really nice fitness center with multiple floors of workout equipment, an indoor track, basketball courts, an indoor pool, etc., but for those people who like a little more privacy, **Barnard offers the same type of equipment on a much smaller scale**."

Q **"Our student center on campus is pretty small,** although they're planning to renovate it soon, but it offers great food, good coffee, mail service, music practice rooms, and a warm, comfortable environment. You can also always go across the street and take advantage of Lerner (Columbia's student center), which has its own movie theater, food services, meeting rooms, etc."

Q "**The best part about our facilities is all the people who run them!** They are awesome, especially Doris, our Goddess in the College Activities Office who leave messages for all her 'strong Barnard Women' on a weekly basis with lots of love and great offers for entertainment."

The College Prowler Take On...
Facilities

As a student on campus at Barnard, you'll be able to take advantage of all the facilities that the Barnard and Columbia University system has to offer. However, you'll find that as a Barnard student living on the west side of Broadway, Barnard's facilities are much more convenient to use. The one exception to this rule is the Dodge Fitness Center, which is Columbia's gym. If you want to workout, then you won't mind walking across the street to Dodge, which is a much better gym than LeFrak, the gym Barnard has to offer. No one really uses LeFrak, except for events such as Midnight Breakfast and for Barnard PE classes, while Dodge offers lots of exercise equipment both in kind and quantity.

Most of Barnard's facilities aren't great and most go unused, with the exception of McIntosh. Columbia's student union, Lerner, is much larger and nicer, which tends to leave Barnard students acutely aware of what they don't have, even though they realize that it's only because Barnard is so much smaller. Most students don't care too much though, because as part of Columbia University they have access to everything on any campus. Whatever kind of facility you're looking to use, it's out there. It might just be a little farther away than you'd like. What really makes Barnard's facilities great, though, are the people that work in each one to make sure that the students are well taken care of, which is something you don't find at too many schools.

B-

The College Prowler™ Grade on

Facilities: B-

A high Facilities grade indicates that the campus is aesthetically pleasing and well-maintained; facilities are state-of-the-art, and libraries are exceptional. Other determining factors include the quality of both athletic and student centers and an abundance of things to do on campus.

Campus Dining

The Lowdown On...
Campus Dining

Freshman Meal Plan Requirement?
Yes

Meal Plan Average Cost:
$2,015 for non-kosher, $2,287 for kosher

Places to Grab a Bite with Your Meal Plan

Hewitt Dining Hall
Location: Basement of Hewitt Hall
Food: Kosher and non-kosher selections of classic American cuisine and some ethnic favorites
Favorite Dish: Sandwiches and salad

Breakfast Hours: Monday through Friday from 8 a.m. to 10 a.m., weekends from 11 a.m. to 2 p.m.

Lunch Hours: Monday though Friday from 11:30 to 2 p.m.

Dinner Hours: Monday though Friday from 5 p.m. to 7:45 pm, weekends from 4:30 to 7 p.m.

Lower Level McIntosh- Home Zone
Location: Lower level of McIntosh Student Center
Food: Comfort Food
Favorite Dish: Meatloaf
Hours: Monday though Friday 11 a.m. to 4 p.m.

➡

Lower Level McIntosh-Pan Geos
Location: Lower level of McIntosh Student Center
Food: Tortilla wraps
Favorite: Vegetarian Wrap
Hours: Monday though Thursday from 11:30 a.m. to 3:30 p.m., Friday from 11 a.m. to 2:30 p.m.

Lower Level McIntosh- Bene Pizzeria
Location: Lower level of McIntosh Student Center
Food: Italian
Favorite: Pizza
Hours: Monday though Friday from 11 a.m. to 4 p.m.

Lower Level McIntosh- The Salad Garden
Location: Lower level of McIntosh Student Center
Food: Salad
Favorite: Build your own salad
Hours: Monday though Friday from 11 a.m. to 4 p.m.

Java City
Location: Upper level of McIntosh Student Center
Food: Breakfast pastries and to-go sandwiches and salads, coffee
Favorite Food: Muffins
Favorite Drink: Chai Tea
Hours: Monday though Thursday 8 a.m. to 12 a.m., Friday from 8 a.m. to 5 p.m., Sunday from 5 p.m. to 12 a.m

Student Favorites:
Hewitt Dining Hall
Lower level Mac

24-Hour On-Campus Eating?
No

Off-Campus Places to Use Your Meal Plan: None

Other Options:
At selected times during the school year, Barnard usually holds events in which the school provides lunch outside for all of its students. At these functions, anyone is welcome to join other teachers, students and administrators for lunch.

Did You Know?

• If you ever have a problem with dining services, or if you just have a request for a certain kind of food, you can **leave a note** on the bulletin board for the managers. They tend to respond quickly by both getting your requested item, if possible, and posting a written response.

Students Speak Out On...
Campus Dining

"The dining halls are not that great, but the food is edible most of the time. Luckily, there are many places to eat out close by. Lower level McIntosh, which uses points, is much better."

Q "In my opinion, the food is excellent in comparison to what I've seen and heard about other campuses. I actually have a friend in Massachusetts who lives on one meal a day because **there's no variety,** so when they make something she doesn't like, she can't eat. And even if you don't like it, you're in the middle of NYC. There's bound to be something open at all hours to satisfy your hunger."

Q "As a transfer and a girl who prefers to eat on my own time, I have never been required to buy a meal plan. **I use the fully functional kitchens**."

Q "The food is good, and they have enough options, but **it can be a bit repetitious if you're kosher** or have other dietary restrictions."

Q "Barnard's main dining areas, Hewitt and McIntosh, offer a good variety of food, especially in comparison to Columbia's main dining area, John Jay Dining Hall. Java City is also until midnight, which can be convenient at times. **The only inconvenience is that Barnard and Columbia have different dining services** so we can't use our 'points' in the other campus dining areas."

Q "**The dining is not the best,** but sometimes you just have to eat."

Q "I actually really enjoy the food on campus. There's usually a pretty good selection to choose from, and they try to cater to all types dining preferences. Hewitt is the Barnard dining hall, but you can also get lunch in lower level Mac. **JJ's Place, at Columbia, offers awesome late night munchies**, including chicken fingers until 2 a.m., and both Java City and Cafe 212 are good for coffee, pastries, etc."

Q "The food on campus is good. Everything is pretty small, but **there are a lot of choices.** Having Tasti D-lite, a low fat, low calorie frozen yogurt place, close by is a plus. The dining halls are pretty good."

Q "The dining halls are decent, but **we're surrounded by good restaurants,** so it usually makes the food seem worse."

Q "The food itself is not bad at all, but once you start to figure out the rotation of entrees, **the magic of 'all you can eat' is quickly gone**."

The College Prowler Take On...
Campus Dining

While there's a lot of discrepancy among Barnard College students, the overwhelming trend is that the food is alright. Although there aren't too many places that are specifically "Barnard" to eat, there's quite a bit of choice at those few places.

On any given day you can find cereal, bacon, eggs, tofu and bagels, among other things, for breakfast and sandwiches, stir-fry, pizza, and meat, vegetarian and vegan entrées for lunch and dinner. There's a kosher section that is set off from the main serving area that serves breakfast, lunch and dinner options. The comments of some Barnard students indicate that some of them are judging Barnard food against other New York City restaurants, and of course the food isn't as good, but it's less than ten dollars for all you can eat. When judging dining hall food, you should always think back to lunch in high school and then appreciate the step up.

Barnard has pretty good food, which your parents will probably note when they help move you in. They, however, will not have to continue eating in Hewitt Dining Hall for the next eight weeks. The entrées that are offered tend to be pretty good for the first few weeks, but quickly become humdrum. The daily pizza selection and sandwich bar can really save some Barnard students from going hungry when the entrée choices don't look good.

One place that dining services at Barnard loses points is in its lack of choice of places to eat. The two dining areas at Barnard are Hewitt Dining Hall, which is located in the basement of Hewitt Hall in the quad, and then the quasi-cafeteria in the lower level of McIntosh. The cafeteria in McIntosh isn't really a cafeteria, but rather a bunch of different food stations together, which is why there isn't a real name for the area. Don't be fooled by the school's website, which lists about six different places to eat. There are really only two.

The College Prowler™ Grade on
Campus Dining: C-

Our grade on Campus Dining addresses the quality of both school-owned dining halls and independent on-campus restaurants as well as the price, availability, and variety of food.

Off-Campus Dining

The Lowdown On...
Off-Campus Dining

Restaurant Prowler:
Popular Places to Eat!

Amir's Falafel
Food: Middle Eastern
Address: 2911 Broadway, Morningside Heights
Phone: (212) 749-7500
Price: Under $10
Hours: Daily 11 a.m.-11p.m.

Awash
Food: Ethiopian, African
Address: 947 Amsterdam Avenue
Phone: (212) 961-1416
Price: Under $15
Hours: Monday through Friday 1 p.m.-12 a.m., Weekends 12 p.m.-12 a.m.

Café con Leche
Food: Cuban, Caribbean, Latin American
Address: 726 Amsterdam Avenue at 95th Street
Phone: (212)-678-7000
Fax: (212) 678-2642
Price: Under $10
Hours: 11 a.m.-11p.m., Brunch: Monday through Friday 11a.m.-4 p.m., Saturday-Sunday 10 a.m.-4 p.m.

Caffe Pertutti
Food: Italian
Address: 2888 Broadway
Phone: (212) 864-1143
Cool Features: Sidewalk Dining
Price: Under $15

Deluxe
Food: American
Address: 2896 Broadway
Phone: (212)662-7900
Cool Features: Sidewalk Dining
Price: Under $10
Hours: Monday through Thursday: 7 a.m.-12 a.m., Friday 7 a.m.-1 a.m., Saturday 8 a.m.-1 a.m., Sunday 8 a.m.-12 a.m.

Famous Famiglia
Food: Italian, Pizza
Address: 2859 Broadway
Phone: (212) 865-1234
Price: Under $15

Flor de Mayo
Food: Latin American, Chinese
Address: 2651 Broadway
Phone: (212) 663-5520
Price: Under $10
Hours: 12 p.m.-12 a.m.

Koronet's
Food: Pizza
Address: 2448 Broadway
Phone: (212) 222-1566
Price: Under $10

La Rosita
Food: Cuban, Caribbean, Latin American
Address: 2809 Broadway
Phone: (212) 663-7804
Price: Under $15
Hours: 7 a.m.- 12:30 a.m.

Lemongrass Grill
Food: Thai
Address: 2534 Broadway
Phone: (212) 666-0888
Price: Under $10

Le Monde
Food: French Bistro
Address: 2885 Broadway
Phone: (212) 531-3939
Cool Features: Sidewalk Dining
Price: Under $15

Metisse
Food: French Bistro
Address: 239 W. 105th Street
Phone: (212) 666-8825
Price: Under $20
Hours: Monday through Thursday: 6:30 p.m.-10:30 p.m., Friday and Saturday: 5:30 p.m.-11 p.m., Sunday: 5:30 p.m.-10 p.m.

Nacho's Kitchen
Food: Mexican Bar and Grill
Address: 2893 Broadway
Phone: (212) 665-2800
Cool Features: Sidewalk Dining
Price: Under $15

Nussbaum and Wu
Food: Bagels and Bakery, Deli
Address: 2897 Broadway
Phone: (212) 280-5344
Fax: (212) 280-5340
Cool Features: Sidewalk Dining
Price: Under $10

Pinnacle
Food: Deli, Bagels, Pizza
Address: 2937 Broadway
Phone: (212) 662-1000
Fax: (212) 662-3828
Price: Under $10

➜

Tom's Diner
Food: Diner, American
Address: 2880 Broadway
Phone: (212) 864-6137
Cool Features: It's the Seinfeld Diner!
Price: Under $10
Hours: 24 hours a day

Tomo
Food: Sushi
Address: 2850 Broadway
Phone: (212) 665-2916
Price: Under $10

Hours: Monday through Saturday: 12 p.m.-11:30 p.m., Sunday: 12 p.m.-11 p.m.

24-Hour Eating:
Tom's Diner

Student Favorites:
Tom's Diner
Ollie's
Koronet
Famiglia
Amir's Falafel

Closest Grocery Stores:
D'Agostino
Broadway & 110th
Upper West Side
(212) 663-9895

Fairway
Riverside & 128th
Harlem
(212) 595-1888

UFM (University Food Market)
Broadway &115th
Morningside Heights

Did You Know?

Best Pizza:
Koronet or Famiglia
Best Chinese:
Swish
Best Breakfast:
Deluxe
Best Bar Food:
The Heights
Best Healthy:

Why eat healthy? What's college without the freshman fifteen?Go with Tomo for some healthy sushi, if you must.

Best Place to Take Your Parents:
Le Monde

Fun Facts
• **Tom's Diner,** located on the corner of 110th and Broadway is famous for being the diner frequented by the characters on the sitcom Seinfeld and the subject of Suzanne Vega's hit song, "Tom's Diner".

Students Speak Out On...
Off-Campus Dining

{ **"The restaurants off campus are diverse in price and type of cuisine. They are also conveniently located."**

Q "There are a lot of restaurants near campus. Nussbaum, Wu and Pertuti are pretty good. **There are also some good kosher restaurants** between 91st and 72nd Street."

Q "There are some good restaurants in the immediate vicinity, but some of them can get kind of expensive. Deluxe has good food. **Their brunch is great**. Pertutti offers good Italian dishes and awesome dessert. Koronet's has the biggest slices of pizza you can get."

Q "**There's a wonderful plethora of restaurants around Barnard located on Broadway**. The most noteworthy of these include Caffé Swish (Pan-Asian), Mill Korean Restaurant, The West End (American), Nacho Mamas (Mexican), Le Monde (French), Tom's Diner, Café Pertutti (Italian), Amir's Falafel (Lebanese), The Heights Bar and Grill, Café Taci (Italian), Pinnacle (twenty-four hour mix of everything), Ollie's(Chinese), Dynasty (Chinese) and my all-time favorite, Koronet's, which has the biggest slices of pizza you'll ever see in your life."

Q "The food nearby campus is decent if you're just hungry, but **you should really go downtown** to some of the more ethnic neighborhoods if you want really great food for a good price. You should use eating as an excuse to explore the city."

Q "**Tom's** near campus is pretty good and they serve food twenty-four hours a day. "

Q "Nacho's is okay and Korean Mill is pretty good. **Tomo's has great Japanese food** and Tom's is fun for late night diner food when nothing else is open. V&T and Max Soha's both have good Italian, and the Hungarian Pastry Shop has a pretty good selection of desserts. For meals on the go, there's Wrapp Factory, Samad's, Nussbaum and Famiglia."

Q "Luckily **there are many off-campus places to eat**—La Rosita is delicious."

Q "There is some pretty good food around campus, but it is very expensive. **Try going a little more downtown** if you can, such as Big Nick's on 77th Street. It is not the best in decor, but there's good food."

Q "There are a wide variety of restaurants to choose from in the Barnard and Columbia neighborhood. Because **Columbia prefers to promote independent businesses,** you won't find a Wendy's or a Burger King. If you're absolutely dying for a Big Mac, the closest MacDonald's is on 125th Street. You can also find a Dunkin' Donuts, a Subway, a Taco Bell and a KFC not far from there."

Q "Since a lot of people like to complain that walking over to Amsterdam is just too far, although in reality it's only one block away, then you may want to try out Symposium, a Greek restaurant on 113th between Amsterdam and Broadway. They have a flaming cheese dish, great gyros and Sangria that could rival a Spanish restaurant. The prices are moderate, and during the summer **they have tables on a little patio in the back."**

Q "If you're not looking to dine in, then you can head over to Samad's, a deli and mini food store, where **all the employees know who you are** and what you want before you open your mouth. They have the absolute best corn chowder I've ever tasted and once they even gave me their own personal recipe. They also have an in-store cat, making your visit all the more memorable."

Q "There are some good places near campus like Pinnacle and Koronet's that are open all night. **Swish has good bubble tea and Tom's is the best diner.** Make sure you try Tomo for sushi."

The College Prowler Take On...
Off-Campus Dining

There is an amazing amount of choice when eating off campus at Barnard, both in the immediate vicinity of the campus and all over New York City. You can find even the most obscure cuisine somewhere in the city. Near Barnard there is a lot of Italian, Chinese and French food, although most restaurants cater to students since they are pretty much the only people that hang out around Columbia and Barnard. Almost all of the restaurants around campus deliver, so when its cold and you don't want to go outside, you can still eat pretty well. Ollie's isn't great in terms of quality of food, but for the price it's a pretty good deal, and Famiglia and Koronet's serve lots of huge, greasy slices of pizza. Deluxe serves the best brunch around. The best restaurant around campus is probably Le Monde because it's close and serves great tasting food. It is a little bit more expensive than the other restaurants nearby, but it's also much nicer inside without being so nice that you would need to change clothes before going to eat there.

The choices that Barnard students have are amazing. The only problem is that choice and quality come at a price, and a lot of times in New York City that price is very high. It's great that Barnard students have so much variability, but it is very frustrating to many people that they can't take advantage of the wide range of dining options because of financial constraints. Although dining hall food is good, it's hard to eat there when all you can think about is sushi or fabulous Italian.

The College Prowler™ Grade on

Off-Campus Dining: A

A high off-campus dining grade implies that off-campus restaurants are affordable, accessible, and worth visiting. Other factors include the variety of cuisine and the availability of alternative options (vegetarian, vegan, Kosher, etc.).

Campus Housing

The Lowdown On...
Campus Housing

Room Types:

Singles, doubles and triples in both a corridor and suite setting.

Best Dorms:

620 W. 116th

Sulzberger Tower

Worst Dorms:

Elliot

Reed

Dormitories

600 W. 116th Street

Floors: 12

Total Occupancy: 161

Bathrooms: One in each suite

Co-Ed: No

Percentage of Men/Women: 0/100

Percentage of First-Year Students: 0

Room Types: Two, four and six person suites made up of doubles and singles

Special Features: Kitchen, laundry, Wellness Floor, hardwood floors and large closets

➔

616 W. 116th Street

Floors: 10

Total Occupancy: 207

Bathrooms: One in each suite

Co-Ed: No

Percentage of Men/Women: 0/100

Percentage of First-Year Students: 0%

Room Types: five and six person suites made up of doubles and singles

Special Features: Laundry room in the basement, fully equipped kitchen in each suite, Wellness Floor, internet access

620 W. 116th Street

Floors: 15

Total Occupancy: 161

Bathrooms: One in each suite

Co-Ed: No

Percentage of Men/Women: 0/100 - This percentage reflects only Barnard students living in this building. Be aware that community tenants also reside here.

Percentage of First-Year Students: 0%

Room Types: Four and five person suites of mostly singles and a few doubles.

Special Features: Laundry room in the basement, fully equipped kitchen in each suite, Wellness Floor, internet access

601 W. 110th

Floors: 8

Total Occupancy: 84

Bathrooms: One or two in each suite

Co-Ed: No, however other community tenants live in this building

Percentage of Men/Women: 0/100

Percentage of First-Year Students: 0%

Room Types: Five and six person suites of doubles and singles

Special Features: Laundry room in the basement, fully equipped kitchen in each suite, internet access

Brooks Hall

Floors: 8

Total Occupancy: 135

Bathrooms: Community, 1 per floor

Co-Ed: No

Percentage of Men/Women: 0/100

Percentage of First-Year Students: 41%

Room Types: Two, four and six person suites of singles, doubles and triples

Special Features: Laundry room in the basements of Hewitt and Sulzberger, Wellness Floor, sinks in some rooms, inoperable fireplaces in some rooms, internet access, first year students live on specific floors

Elliot Hall

Floors: 6

Total Occupancy: 131

Bathrooms: One community bathroom in each suite

Co-Ed: No

Percentage of Men/Women: 0/100

Percentage of First-Year Students: 0%

Room Types: Twelve person suites in a corridor style made up of doubles and singles

Special Features: Laundry room in the basement, kitchen in each suite, Wellness Floor, internet access

Hewitt Hall

Floors: 8

Total Occupancy: 235

Bathrooms: Community

Co-Ed: No

Percentage of Men/Women: 0/100

Percentage of First-Year Students: 0

Room Types: Two, four and six person suites

Special Features: Laundry room in the basement, fully equipped kitchen in each suite, Wellness Floor, first year students live on specific floors

Plimpton Hall

Floors: 15

Total Occupancy: 280

Bathrooms: Private bath in each suite

Co-Ed: No

Percentage of Men/Women: 0/100

Percentage of First-Year Students: 0

Room Types: Five single rooms per suite

Special Features: Laundry room in the basement, fully equipped kitchen in each suite, Wellness Floor, Piano, ping-pong and pool tables

Reid Hall

Floors: 8

Total Occupancy: 275

Bathrooms: Community

Co-Ed: No

Percentage of Men/Women: 0/100

Percentage of First-Year Students: 100%

Room Types: Corridor style consisting of doubles

Special Features: Wellness Floor

Room Types: Split Double, Single, Corner Suite

Special Features: Branch of SU Bookstore, Garage, Computer Cluster, Meeting Room, Laundry, TV Lounge

S

Sulzberger Tower

Floors: 16

Total Occupancy: 124

Bathrooms: Private bath in each suite

Co-Ed: No

Percentage of Men/Women: 0/100

Percentage of First-Year Students: 100%

Room Types: Eight people to a suite of singles and doubles

Special Features: Laundry, kitchen, Wellness Floor, upper floors have views of the city skyline, first year students live on specific floors, only upper classmen are allowed in singles

Number of Dormitories:
10

Undergrads on Campus:
2,185

University-Owned Apartments:
4

Bed Type
Extra long twin

Available for Rent
Barnard does not specifically rent out refrigerators or other appliances like that, but there are always people on campus during move in time that do.

Cleaning Service?
Community restrooms and public areas are cleaned. The rest is up to the students using them.

What You Get
Each student receives a Bed, desk, desk chair, bookshelf and a wardrobe for each room. Suites with kitchens are equipped with a stove, oven and refrigerator.

Also Available:
All dormitories are smoke-free, but there are several special-interest housing options such as wellness floors, where no one smokes or drinks.

Did You Know?

- Some of the older dormitory rooms come with **hardwood floors,** fireplaces and/or sinks in the room.

Students Speak Out On...
Campus Housing

> **"Dorms are nice for the city. Avoid Elliott and most Quad singles and go for the 600s or 110th Street instead."**

Q "The dorms are nice, well at least some of them. If living on the quad, then Sulzberger is definitely the best because the rooms are larger and there is air conditioning. **I would not want to live in Brooks**, though, because I don't think I could live with three other people."

Q "Dorms are generally pretty nice. **The quad is good if you're looking for hall style living**. You're required to live there your first year, but there are always really great options off campus, but still within the realm of college housing."

Q "**Most dorms are nice**. Sulzberger, which is for freshmen only, has air-conditioning and a lot of the dorms went under renovation recently. The 600s suites are said to be very nice and accounts for the fact that upperclassmen get priority when it comes to housing."

Q "The dorms are pretty good compared to those of other colleges I've seen in NYC. Most girls get to live in singles by their second year, while in other colleges people don't get singles until their senior year.All the dorms are great, so it's personal choice and quality is not a concern in this case. **You might want to avoid 110th Street** just because it's farther away from campus, but if you don't mind that, it's okay."

Q "The dorms are alright. **The 600s are the best places to live,** like 600, 616 and 620. Avoid Elliott because it has very small rooms and the Quad after the first year, because there are much nicer places to live."

Q "One-hundred and tenth Street is a hidden gem—it's six blocks from Barnard, but **the walk is actually really nice and easy,** and you can't beat the apartment style experience you get there. People interested in singles always have options in Elliot, Plimpton or the Quad, and I've heard pretty good things about 616 and 600."

Q "Many students will agree that the one thing that can potentially put a damper on a Barnard girl's college experience is the poor condition of the dorms. **In all the places I've lived there have been problems with everything from vermin, walls in dire need of a new paint job, plumbing, fuses blowing and cramped spaces.** Part of this is because we are located in New York City, a place notorious for its rundown apartments and sky-high rent. At the same time, one would hope that Barnard's facilities would actually take the time to clean the dorms before students move into them in the fall. Since this is not usually the case, bring a mop, a broom, a good scrubbing brush, some Comet and get to work."

Q "Because first-year students are required to have a meal plan, they all live in what we call 'The Quad', a series of four buildings connected in a square. Of these four dorms, **the most desirable by far is Sulzberger,** the newest and cleanest of the dorms. Reid, a building only for freshmen, is probably the second cleanest, although when I lived there the bathrooms were dirty and in need of renovation. Brooks and Hewitt are the oldest and most run-down. While they have tried to fix up Hewitt, a dorm that consists mostly of singles and is home to many sophomores, they painted the halls in bright neon colors that make you feel like you're in a circus."

Q "Brooks is the least desirable of the four because there is not a lot of privacy and **the doubles are tiny.** On the occasions when I lived in Brooks and Hewitt, vermin were also an issue. Also, make sure you bring lots of extension cords. In Hewitt there was only one outlet per room."

The College Prowler Take On...
Campus Housing

If you choose to live on campus at Barnard there are several housing styles to choose from, and after your first year on campus you may select housing based on what style appeals to you. For many college students, privacy is the most important aspect of housing. Those students might choose a suite in 620, or a single in Elliot or the Quad. For students with a more social environment in mind, 616, 600 or a room in the campus owned apartments might be the best bet. Another consideration is how independent you want to be from the college scene.

Many people in college may enjoy a traditional corridor style of living for their first few years, but then may want a more independent lifestyle as they near graduation. As you move to addresses further away from the college's physical location, you will find that you are no longer required to purchase a meal plan, get rooms with kitchens, private baths and sitting rooms, and live in settings that are no longer college dorms, but regular apartments. One of the few problems with the range of housing that is offered is that while there's something for everyone at Barnard, the chances of a person getting matched up with their dream room is pretty slim. Another problem is that some housing options are a little bit far from campus, so while a person may be able to find a room that they like, they may not be able to find one that is very close to campus.

One very important thing to keep in mind at Barnard is that some of the rooms and suites are very old, so there are a lot of exposed pipes and some rooms with very strange, small dimensions. On the other hand, old also brings a lot of charm to some of the rooms that feature hardwood floors and fireplaces.

B

The College Prowler™ Grade on
Campus Housing: B

A high Campus Housing grade indicates that dorms are clean, well-maintained, and spacious. Other determining factors include variety of dorms, proximity to classes, and social atmosphere.

Off-Campus Housing

The Lowdown On...
Off-Campus Housing

Undergrads in Off-Campus Housing:
10%

Average Rent for a Studio:
$1,500/month

Average Rent for a 1BR:
$2,500/month

Average Rent for a 2BR:
$3,000/month

Best Time to Look for a Place
At the end of the spring semester or the beginning of the fall semester

Popular Areas:
Morningside Heights
Upper West Side

For Assistance Contact:
Residence Life

Web: http://www.barnard.edu/offcampus/reslife/index.html

Phone: (212) 854-1561

E-mail: housing@barnard.edu

Students Speak Out On...
Off-Campus Housing

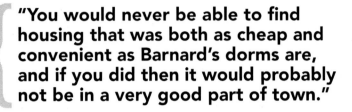

"You would never be able to find housing that was both as cheap and convenient as Barnard's dorms are, and if you did then it would probably not be in a very good part of town."

Q "Off-campus housing has its pluses and minuses. **If you don't mind the walk, then it's fine.** Depending on which suite you get it is definitely worth it. If anything there are always singles located in the quad."

Q "I live at 110th Street, which is off campus, but still considered college housing and I love it. I can't say enough about it. As for off-campus housing, I really don't know much. My guess is that **apartments in the area are pretty expensive,** so you're probably better off in the housing lottery with Barnard."

Q "There is always NYC transportation to get people to places. However, if you were to drive, they'd find a lot of difficulty finding free parking. **There are many nice places to live,** but they're expensive."

Q "Off-campus housing depends where you are commuting from. **If you live far away, it isn't worth it** because you sometimes might have to make two trips to school in one day for some reason and it'll take too much time. I commuted last year, but I lived close by so it wasn't inconvenient at all. Barnard really tries to accommodate commuters with a commuter lounge, special activities, etc."

Q "**I don't really know anyone that lives off campus**. I wouldn't do it until at least after sophomore year so you could meet people, otherwise it might be hard to get involved at school."

Q "I think the only people who really live off campus are **girls who live at home to save money**."

Q "Housing off campus **doesn't seem worth it to me**. It's New York City and everything is really expensive."

The College Prowler Take On...
Off-Campus Housing

There are some beautiful places to live off-campus, and pretty much anyone can imagine themselves living across the street from Central Park with skyline views. However, not many people, not to mention college students, can afford this. Apartments in New York are very expensive, and unless you're one of those lucky people who can afford this type of luxury, living off-campus is probably not the best idea.

When talking with Barnard students, it is sometimes difficult to discern what "off-campus" housing is. Some students consider it to be housing that's owned by the college and is located far away, while others view it as non-college owned property. Morningside Heights is a very nice area to live in and is very convenient for involvement on campus and going to class, but prices in this area are a little bit high.

The next most obvious choice would be to look for a place in a nearby neighborhood, however outside of Morningside Heights the prices tend to be even higher, or the neighborhood isn't in a great area. But, people do find housing off campus and are usually very happy with it. This often happens when a group of people are able to find a good deal in Morningside Heights. If you can find a good deal, it might be worth it to you, but do keep in mind that housing on campus comes in all varieties, so it's worth checking out all your options. Getting housing through the school can be cheaper and just less of a hassle.

D-

The College Prowler™ Grade on

Off-Campus Housing: D-

A high grade in Off-Campus Housing indicates that apartments are of high quality, close to campus, affordable, and easy to secure.

Diversity

The Lowdown On...
Diversity

American Indian:
1%

Asian or Pacific Islander:
19%

African American:
5%

Hispanic:
6%

White:
65%

International:
3%

Unknown:
1%

Out of State:
64%

Political Activity

Not everyone on campus is active politically, but those who are, are very visible. Expect to have to defend your political stance if you voice it on campus. The campus always becomes more politically "charged" around presidential election years, but you can always find some ideological company in the Republican, Democratic, etc. Clubs no matter when you're looking to get involved.

Gay Tolerance

Barnard is very gay tolerant and the gay community tends to be relatively visible on campus. Their relationship with the straight community is one that indicates that sexual orientation is not divisive on campus.

Most Popular Religions

There is a large Jewish population at Barnard that is very visible and tends to stick together. Christianity is also popular in terms of numbers; however, their religious presence is not felt on campus as much as the Jewish presence is.

Economic Status

Although there is a large economic range when it comes to Barnard students, the trend is overwhelming more affluent. There are a few girls that come from more of a modest upbringing, but most are either wealthy or pretend to be.

Minority Clubs

Although many Barnard students complain about the lack of diversity, there are quite a few minority clubs. You really don't hear about them doing too much during the school year, except for a small event here and there. The clubs you hear about most often are Latina clubs, who tend to be quite active despite their relative small proportion on campus.

Students Speak Out On...
Diversity

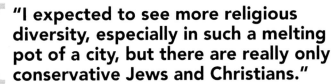

"I expected to see more religious diversity, especially in such a melting pot of a city, but there are really only conservative Jews and Christians."

Q "It is **more diverse than most Ivy Leagues,** but then again their diversity is so low that can't say much about this campus."

Q "**It's pretty diverse**—politically, racially, religiously, etc."

Q "**I wish there was more diversity** just so I could be exposed to more things, but I'm sure even if every race was equally represented there still would be ethnic cliques."

Q "The campus is **not as diverse as I'd like it to be.**"

Q "I think the campus is pretty diverse. **You see a lot of Asians and Blacks on campus**, although you don't see nearly as many Hispanics."

Q "Barnard's campus, from what I've seen, **is not very diverse in terms of different ethnicities.** I find that there are not many Blacks, Hispanics or Asians. However, Columbia is a little more diverse."

Q "My first roommate was not only my same ethnicity and religion, but also from the same state and a town very near my hometown. We were put together because they thought we might have something in common. **I'm not really sure if Barnard is bothering with diversity.**"

Q "One of the most valuable things I have learned out here is to **maximize the benefits of diversity**. We all have so much to learn from each other."

The College Prowler Take On...
Diversity

For a college that's ranked eighth in US News and World Report for diversity on campus, you'd really think you'd see more of it on campus. Of course, everyone realizes that Barnard doesn't have a large student body, so ethnic diversity in small numbers counts for a lot. However, there's not much political or religious diversity to be seen on campus, and one might argue that this is just as important as ethnic diversity when it comes to the enrichment of students' lives on campus.

The key reason for diversity on campus is that it brings groups together for different causes, like republicans and democrats conversing because of their religious or ethnic commonalities. Just like many other schools, Barnard has many people of different races and cultures, but for the most part these people tend to stick together.It's great that there's diversity on campus, but there's no point in having it if no one mingles. It's really not fair that the school is looked down upon for this when ultimately it's the reposibility of the students' to get involved with diverse groups on campus. Barnard does try to foster diversity on campus, especially ethnic diversity with groups, with organizations such as the McIntosh Activities Council's Multicultural Committee which puts on the One World show each year. Overall, Barnard does try to be very diverse. It's just the students who don't cooperate that give the college a sort of clique-ish feel.

B-

The College Prowler™ Grade on
Diversity: B-

A high grade in Diversity indicates that ethnic minorities and international students have a notable presence on campus and that students of different economic backgrounds, religious beliefs, and sexual preferences are well-represented.

Guys & Girls

The Lowdown On...
Guys & Girls

Men Undergrads:	Women Undergrads:
0	2,297

Birth Control Available?

Yes, many forms of birth control are available such as the pill, the patch, the morning after pill, the ring and the shot, all for very reasonable prices. Condoms and dental dams are also available free of charge.

Social Scene:

When Barnard girls go out, they tend to go downtown and far away from the college scene. Just like in any other college town, the bars will card pretty tough right around campus, although it's usually easier for a girl to get the man at the door to look the other way. To avoid this, Barnard girls will go downtown where the crowd is a little less juvenile.

simply hang in the dorm on the weekends.

Hookups or Relationships?

There is a saying around the Columbia University community that says, "Columbia to wed; Barnard to bed". This isn't entirely warranted, but there is a little bit of truth to it. Either a Barnard girl has a long distance boyfriend or she is going from guy-to-guy, though not necessarily a Columbia guy because most of them are stuck-up and far fewer are good looking.

Best Place to Meet Guys/Girls:

The best place to meet someone is in class or some sort of club involvement, if you really want to be interested in them as a person. Otherwise, go to bars. There are lots of guys and girls there that only come to talk to and hit on other guys and girls, especially at the West End. Set your standards low and you won't be disappointed.

Did You Know?
Top Places to Find Hotties:
1. Dodge Fitness Center
2. The West End
3. In Class

Top Places to Hookup:
1. The West End
2. Any of the Many Single Dorm Rooms
3. Dodge Fitness Center
4. The Heights
5. Butler Library at Columbia

Dress Code

You get everything at Barnard. Girls come to class wearing everything from sweatpants and a tank top to stilettos. This isn't a dressy school by any means, so although it isn't strange to see a classmate in office attire, there isn't any need to dress that way. In fact, in the mornings, there is always that one person that comes down to breakfast in their pajamas and robe. In hand with the Jewish presence at Barnard, you will see a lot of long skirts. New York is fashion forward, but you don't have to be.

Students Speak Out On...
Guys & Girls

> "It's an all-girls school—what more can I say? And the guys at Columbia aren't that good looking to say the least."

Q "**Most of the girls are average looking**, but there are a few that you can really tell have money."

Q "Beauty is in the eye of the beholder. I suppose **it depends on your definition of 'hot',** but I think there's a pretty fair selection here."

Q "**The guys are all very intelligent,** so while you may not get the hottest guys, you'll still have the smartest and you'll admire them for that. There are of course some hot guys because there are many schools in the university that there's bound to be a few hot guys occasionally."

Q "Columbia guys can be either arrogant or just totally unaware of girls around them because their nose is in a book. **Columbia girls either don't care at all whether a girl is from Barnard or Columbia,** or they absolutely hate Barnard girls for taking their guys."

Q "**A lot of people think Barnard is a school for lesbians,** but there really aren't very many that go here. Mostly students either date Columbia guys or have long distance relationships from home."

Q "The good looking guys are few and far between, especially the available nice ones, but **the girls are awesome!** Of course we're hot."

Q "Most of the students here have come from relatively privileged backgrounds so they are highly able to take care of themselves. On the other hand, **it seems that many of them get to be arrogant and sheltered**. But for the most part, most of the people are very congenial and friendly, as well as witty and learned."

Q "There's a wide variety of people that go to both Columbia and Barnard. **Of course, since Barnard is all girls, there are no guys.** However, there are guys in the classes. Cross-registration is allowed, so you can take classes at Columbia and Columbia guys take classes at Barnard. So, it's not like you won't ever see guys."

The College Prowler Take On...
Guys & Girls

Looks rate very low on the priority list for girls at Barnard. Some people will come to class in an outfit very similar to the one they wore to bed the night before. When sleep is precious, and you're not trying to impress anyone, then what you wear to class doesn't matter. Other people, however, might show up in a dress and heels to class. This usually isn't because they want to look good, but usually because they have a fantastic interview downtown that they need to look the part for. The main theme for Barnard girls is that they don't try to look a certain way for looks sake, but rather for the weather, for a job, or because they're tired and they're going right back to sleep after class.

As far as strict looks go, there are some truly beautiful women that attend Barnard. The dancers in particular are usually quite gorgeous. However, there are quite a few more that aren't so aesthetically blessed. Barnard is a college to be yourself; so even the ugliest of ducklings wouldn't feel left out because they don't have flawless skin or straight, gleaming teeth. People might come to Barnard for a lot of things, but they don't come to run with a crowd of supermodels. It's not that Barnard women aren't attractive; it's that they realize how many things are more important than their appearance. They're in college to expand their mind, not spend every minute fixing their hair and looking in the mirror.

The College Prowler™ Grade on
Girls: B+

A high grade for Guys indicates that the male population on campus is attractive, smart, friendly, and engaging, and that the school has a decent ratio of guys to girls.

 B+

Athletics

The Lowdown On...
Athletics

Athletic Division:
NCAA/ I-AA

Conference:
Ivy League

Number of female undergraduate varsity athletes: 336

Women's Teams:
Archery
Basketball
Crew
Field Hockey
Lacrosse
Golf
Soccer
Softball
Swimming
Tennis
Track & Field
Volleyball
Field Hockey

→

Club Sports:

Akido
Archery
Badminton
Ballroom Dance
Boxing
Brazilian Ju Jitsu
Capoeira,
Cricket
Cycling
Equestrian
Figure Skating
Field Hockey
Go Ju Ryo Karate
Hiking
Hockey
Karate
Judo
Kayak
Kendo
Kickboxing
Kung Fu
Lacrosse
Racquetball
Road Runners
Rugby
Sailing
Shotokan Karate
Skiing
Squash
Swing Dance
Table Tennis
Tae Chi Chuan
Tae Kwon Do
Ultimate Frisbee
Volleyball
Water Polo

Intramurals:

Akido
Archery
Badminton
Ballroom Dance
Boxing
Brazilian Ju Jitsu
Capoeira,
Cricket
Cycling
Equestrian
Figure Skating
Field Hockey
Go Ju Ryo Karate
Hiking
Hockey
Karate
Judo
Kayak
Kendo
Kickboxing
Kung Fu
Lacrosse
Racquetball
Road Runners
Rugby
Sailing
Shotokan Karate
Skiing
Squash
Swing Dance
Table Tennis
Tae Chi Chuan
Tae Kwon Do
Ultimate Frisbee
Volleyball
Water Polo

Athletic Fields

Baker Field
Andy Coakley Field
Columbia Soccer Field

School Mascot

Bear

Getting Tickets

Columbia/Barnard sports are not very popular and getting tickets is usually quite easy. They can be purchased online at http://www.gocolumbialions.com/comm/tickets.html or by calling the ticket office at (212) 854-2546.

Most Popular Sports

Football, Basketball

Overlooked Teams:

Track & Field, Soccer

Best Place to Take a Walk

Riverside Park

Gyms/Facilities

Barnard Dance Annex- Barnard is very proud of its dance program and, because of the high demand for classes, has part of a building dedicated to it. The facilities are set up as classrooms, and while they are not the most state of the art, they are much nicer than what most colleges would devote to them.

Dodge Fitness Center- Everything is located at Dodge, from the stairmasters to the indoor track to the competition gym. Look for class postings which offer semester long classes like Brazilian Jujitsu for quite a steal. There is always room for improvement, but Dodge is by far the best gym Barnard students have to choose from.

LeFrak Gymnasium- LeFrak is Barnard's gym which boasts a small weigh facility and an indoor track. The gym is there for anyone one to use, but most people only go inside for large events like Midnight Breakfast.

Students Speak Out On...
Athletics

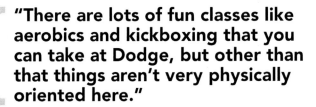

"There are lots of fun classes like aerobics and kickboxing that you can take at Dodge, but other than that things aren't very physically oriented here."

Q "**No one is very interested in sports** because they take up so much time. Most people can't afford to stay out every night playing basketball."

Q "Basketball got really big this year thanks to Coach Joe Jones, but athletics don't typically get that much attention. Football could be big, but the field is kind of out of the way, so a lot of people are kind of oblivious to it. Basketball games are really fun though, and everyone gets really into them, so **they're great to go to if you want to see Columbia school spirit in action.** Football could get bigger next year. I hear rumors of Football Mania coming to campus, so maybe there'll be some more games to get excited about".

Q "I never hear about any of the sports. **I wouldn't know when a game was even going on.**"

Q "Sports take up a pretty large part of Columbia's activities. **There are lots of intramural games** like basketball at Barnard and Columbia."

Q "Sports are not big at all. There isn't a huge fan base at sporting events. **Quite a few people play Intramural sports**, but that's not huge either."

Q "Varsity and Intramural **sports aren't the highest priority** at Columbia University, but they're still a lot of fun to be a part of."

Q "Either you're into sports here because you know someone on the team or you're not. **There are a few people who know everything that goes on**, but the rest of the college has no idea."

The College Prowler Take On...
Athletics

Through the Barnard/Columbia Consortium, Barnard girls play varsity and club sports on Columbia's teams, which affords them the opportunity to compete on a larger scale than they would if Barnard had its own teams. This isn't a huge deal, however, because Columbia's sports aren't good at all and no one watches them. You could ask twenty Barnard students what the score was at the Columbia football game and not a single person would be able to tell you. In fact, most students can't name anyone on any of the varsity teams, or tell you where the field is or what it's called. The athletic offices always make claims that Columbia is going to come back, or that this year will be the big year, but student just don't take them seriously. There's just so much to do in New York that Barnard students don't have time for college football at a stadium that's nowhere near campus.

Playing sports and being active is great, so many people take advantage of the club and intramural sports, but very few can, or want to afford the time commitment that varsity sports demand, especially for teams that aren't very good. The sports facilities could be better, but it's easy to see why the administration wouldn't want to put money into something that students aren't really that interested in anyway. At Barnard you can find ways to get involved with athletics and be active, especially on a non-competitive level, but just don't expect to go cheer for the team at Homecoming.

The College Prowler™ Grade on

Athletics: D-

A high grade in Athletics indicates that students have school spirit, that sports programs are respected, that games are well-attended, and that intramurals are a prominent part of student life.

Nightlife

The Lowdown On...
Nightlife

Club Prowler:
Popular Nightlife Spots!

The area immediately surrounding campus is totally devoid of anything except bars in terms of nightlife, but being in New York City nothing is very far away. If you don't mind making a trip downtown you can have your pick from the swankest, celebrity studded clubs in town. The clubs are there. All you have to do is get in.

Avalon

47 W. 20th Street, Chelsea

Avalon is a strict dress-to-impress club that is eighteen and over on Fridays and twenty-one and older on Saturdays. It welcomes the very biggest names in progressive techno and trance. Show up dressed to the nines and with a large group of girls if you want to get in.

Copacabana

617 W. 57th Street, Midtown
 (212) 582-2672

Copacabana is a twenty-one and over club with fabulous live Latin music.

Exit

610 W. 56th St, Midtown

(212) 582-8282

Exit is a huge club that plays all kinds of music from dance to R&B. Come dressed nicely if you want to party here.

The Roxy

515 W. 18th Street, Chelsea

(212) 645-5156

The Roxy can get quite expensive, and depending on what night you go, you can get vastly different scenes. The Roxy often hosts some of the biggest names in trance and techno music, but also boasts the "biggest, most gay party in New York".

Sound Factory

618 W. 46th Street, Midtown

 (212) 489-0001

Sound Factory is a nice, dressy club that spins progressive techno until seven in the morning.

Bar Prowler:

Like the clubs, Barnard and New York City offer a wide variety of bars for you to choose from. Whatever your style, you're sure to find a place that suits you.

The Abbey Pub

237 W. 105th

(212) 222-8713

The Abbey Pub can get a little bit loud on game days.

The Heights

2867 Broadway, Morningside Heights

(212) 886-7035

The Heights has a smaller, more person feel than The West End in a small bar and grill a couple floors above Broadway. Check out the Happy Hour everyday from 5 p.m. to 7 p.m. on the roof.

SoHa

988 Amsterdam

(212) 678-0098

A small dark bar with fairly decent food.

Tap-a-Keg

2731 Broadway

(212) 749-1734

Tap-a-Keg is a fun dive bar with a seven hour long happy hour. Check out their kitsch, low ceilings and linoleum floors.

The West End

2911 Broadway, Morningside Heights

(212)662-8830

The West End is a mainstay for Barnard and Columbia students. There is always a crowd there almost every night of the week. Make sure to grab a cheap pitcher of beer. This is the best place to meet up with tons of freshmen and kids from other New York schools looking to hook up.

Bars Close At:
2 a.m.

Cheapest Place to Get a Drink:
West End

Student Favorites
The West End, The Heights, Cannon's Pub

Primary Areas with Nightlife:
Bleeker Street
Mulberry Street
Broadway between
113th and 110th
Anywhere downtown

Local Specialties:
Like most schools, we make fabulous trashcan punch.

Other Places to Check Out:
Everywhere else in the city.

Useful Resources for Nightlife
If you are having trouble with any of these sources you can always just check the bills posted on construction sites.

What to Do if You're Not 21
Find some older friends and go out anyways. Most bars and clubs in New York won't turn away a girl, especially if she is dressed nicely and is over eighteen.

Organization Parties:
It's unheard of for the school to sponsor a party with alcohol. This just doesn't ever happen. Other clubs will throw parties, like Orgo on the night before Organic Chemistry finals, but if you want a party, you shouldn't be looking on campus.

Favorite Drinking Games:
Beer Pong, Card Games (A$$hole), Century Club, Quarters Power Hour

Students Speak Out On...
Nightlife

"Go out downtown if you really want to have a blast. It's super expensive, but definitely worth it."

"Parties on campus are okay. Depending on what night you go, and if you have an ID, **the clubs are really great**. Barnard students have a variety to choose from in the city. I like going to Copacabana."

"It's so expensive to go out in the city. **You can only go out like once a month unless you're rich**. I've been to clubs in New York that sell bottles of water for eight dollars, and these are the same bottles you can buy for sixty-five cents in a vending machine!"

"Typically, **everyone hangs out at the West End**. It's not the most exciting bar in the world, but most people just go there for the company anyway. A good crowd is always guaranteed on the weekends and some weekdays, and it's pretty easy to get in, so that's probably your best bet. In addition to West End, there's always Cannon's Pub. A lot of people like The Heights or AmCaf, and if all else fails, there's always Nacho's. For the more adventurous, there are some pretty great clubs outside of the Morningside Heights area, but you have to be willing to look."

"Tons of people go to the West End. It's pretty much just a college bar. It's nothing special and it's always crowded. **There's a lot to do,** just nothing very close to Barnard."

"Parties on campus are few and far between, but **the bar and club scene is awesome**, although it gets expensive."

www.collegeprowler.com

Q "From what I have experienced, there is not too many parties on campus in comparison to other party schools. However, **there are parties in the college bars around campus**. And of course you're in NYC so any club or lounge will always offer some sort of entertainment."

Q "In New York, you should always be able to find a place to have some fun at night. **The area around Barnard is just bars** though, so you would probably want to go downtown."

The College Prowler Take On...
Nightlife

There are few places in the world with nightlife as abundant as in New York City. Unfortunately, all of this fantastic nightlife is far from Barnard's campus. Since Barnard and Columbia make up almost all of Morningside Heights, there are plenty of places to find liquor nearby, but these places just provide the drinks and forget about the ambience. This probably isn't very different than other college towns, but because New York has so much more to offer, students know that the bar scene is lacking. Most of the time students don't really care and enjoy just hanging out with friends over few drinks near campus, and appreciate that they don't have to pay a cab fare or the high prices for Manhattan's trendy drinks.

There are plenty of bars to choose from on Broadway near Barnard, but because there is far less space than there are students, they tend to be crowded no matter when you go. There are no clubs near Barnard at all, which is fine since clubbing is so expensive anyway. Most people don't mind spending twelve dollars on a cab to get downtown when the club's cover is $30. Basically, there is any sort of entertainment you could ever imagine in New York, but for Barnard students it's more of a question of money and motivation. You'll probably usually want cheap and convenient, but if you ever feel the need to do something special, and go to one of the many clubs or bars downtown, you're sure to have a good time. There are dozens of places just a cab ride and cover charge away.

The College Prowler™ Grade on

Nightlife: A

A high grade in Nightlife indicates that there are many bars and clubs in the area that are easily accessible and affordable. Other determining factors include the number of options for the under-21 crowd and the prevalence of house parties.

Greek Life

The Lowdown On...
Greek Life

Number of Fraternities:
6

Number of Sororities:
4

Fraternities on Campus:
Delta Sigma Phi
Pi Kappa Alpha
Sigma Chi
Sigma Nu
Sigma Phi Epsilon
Zeta Psi

Sororities on Campus:
Alpha Chi Omega
Delta Gamma
Kappa Alpha Theta
Sigma Delta Tau

Multicultural Colonies:

Alpha Kappa Alpha

Kappa Phi Lambda

Lambda Phi Epsilon

Phi Iota Alpha

Sigma Iota Alpha

Sigma Lambda Upsilon

Other Greek Organizations:

Greek Council

Greek Peer Advisors

Interfraternity Council

Order of Omega

Panhellenic Council

Did You Know?

• Every year during **Greek Week** fraternities and sororities get together all over campus to play outdoor games.

• Greek Row is not on a street of large houses at Columbia/Barnard like it is at many other colleges, but is instead on a street of **Brownstone row houses.**

Students Speak Out On...
Greek Life

> "So far I've only met one girl that's in a sorority at Barnard, but the Columbia guys that are in the frats seem like the stupid ones that got in because they've got money or something."

○ "**You don't see Greek life at all,** although I do have friends who belong to them and love them."

○ "**Barnard doesn't really have a Greek scene.** It's not like at other places where there is the hot sorority and the girl-next-door sorority. There are just a few, and you don't ever hear about them."

○ "Greek life does exist, but **it's not as prominent here** as it is on some other campuses. Parties happen occasionally, but the social scene is really more dependent on bars and clubs than on frats and sororities."

○ "**It's so sad.** You can't even tell when rush week is here."

○ "**It exists but doesn't dominate the social scene.** I don't really know because I'm not part of a sorority."

○ "**Greek life, what's that?** We only see it during 'Greek Week', unless you're into that sort of thing."

Q "Greek life at Barnard **is a joke** compared to what it is at other schools. My roommate was pledging and she didn't even go to all the events and was still allowed in. So few people care here that sororities can't be selective at all. They just have to keep letting people in to stay alive."

85 www.collegeprowler.com

The College Prowler Take On...
Greek Life

Most people could maybe name one sorority on campus, which puts Greek life at only a slightly better place than Columbia football. A few of the girls on campus that belong to sororities look the part, but mostly you can't tell who is who. It's not like other schools where certain 'types' of girls join certain sororities. They all just kind of blend in by being equally unknown. There are more "I love New York" shirts on campus than Greek ones. In fact, the only way some people know that Barnard/Columbia even has a Greek system is Greek Week, which is a week in which all the organizations get together and compete in games all over campus.

The best thing about Greek life on campus is their sorority and fraternity houses, which are nothing at all like the large traditional looking houses you find at other schools. At Barnard/Columbia Greek Row is on the south side of campus and is made up of brownstones, which is also a testament to their tiny size. The people who are involved in sororities and fraternities are very involved, but most people just don't join a Greek organization, partially because of the expense and also because you just don't hear how to go about getting in. I mean, I'm sure that if you really wanted to join a sorority for some reason you'd be able to figure out what you have to do to pledge, but so few people are involved in Greek life here—I don't know why you'd want to join anyway.

The College Prowler™ Grade on

Greek Life: C-

A high grade in Greek Life indicates that sororities and fraternities are not only present, but also active on campus. Other determining factors include the variety of houses available and the respect the Greek community receives from the rest of the campus.

Drug Scene

The Lowdown On...
Drug Scene

Most Prevalent Drugs on Campus:
Marijuana
Ecstasy
Adderall

Liquor-Related Referrals:
32

Liquor-Related Arrests:
0

Drug-Related Referrals:
0

Drug-Related Arrests:
0

Drug Counseling Programs
ASAP, Alcohol Substance Awareness Program-Students may elect to join this program on their own or may be assigned to it if they are caught using substances illegally

Students Speak Out On...
Drug Scene

"Alcohol and smoking is prevalent, as the situation is with most other campuses. However, partying at Barnard is not excessive."

Q "**I don't think people at Barnard do drugs** in the conventional sense. You don't really ever hear of anyone looking for drugs or worrying about being caught for using them."

Q "**People do drugs and drink,** but no more than any other college."

Q "Most people at Barnard have probably tried drugs at one point, but **there are no real drug users here.**"

Q "People drink and stuff like that, but **no one really does bad drugs.**"

Q "Girls at Barnard will probably say that there are no drugs on campus. There aren't drugs like heroin or anything, but **there's a lot of prescription sharing** and taking legal prescriptions illegally."

Q "Barnard girls just aren't the type to take anything. **I can't imagine anyone here having a problem with things like that.**"

Q "I'm not sure what the drug scene is like here. **I don't do that sort of thing** nor does anyone I know here."

The College Prowler Take On...
Drug Scene

It is possible to graduate from Barnard without ever seeing someone on drugs, taking drugs, or talking about taking drugs. They're just something that people who go to Barnard don't mess with, usually because most of the students were never exposed to that sort of scene. New York City and even the area right outside of Barnard are crawling with drugs, and most students know that should they ever want to try any sort of drug that they will be able to find it with relative ease. The most common drugs on campus are either drugs that enhance a party like ecstasy, drugs that help reduce stress, like marijuana, alcohol or nicotine, or prescription drugs like Adderall to help students stay awake to study.

It's not like Barnard really has to do anything to keep drugs off campus. The school is really kind of made up of kids who want to be in school working hard, as opposed to kids whose parents made them go to college. Most of the girls at Barnard have a very specific agenda and won't be deterred by fleeting things like drugs. The only type of drugs that anyone at Barnard might use would be awareness enhancers to help with staying awake or studying, but that isn't even very prevalent either. All things considered, there isn't really a drug scene at Barnard. If you are into drugs, you'll be able to find them, but you probably won't want to because no one else will be doing them, and there's so much else going on.

The College Prowler™ Grade on
Drug Scene:A-

A high grade in the Drug Scene indicates that drugs are not a noticeable part of campus life; drug use is not visible, and no pressure to use them seems to exist.

Campus Strictness

The Lowdown On...
Campus Strictness

What Are You Most Likely to Get Caught Doing on Campus?

- Keeping candles or other forbidden decorations in your room
- Parking illegally
- Underage drinking
- Drug use

"I think Barnard realizes that as long as students aren't hurting themselves or other people they should leave them alone. People break rules all the time, but that doesn't mean the college shouldn't still have them."

○ "Barnard is pretty strict about drugs and drinking in dorms. **However, lots of drinking goes on** all around Columbia and Barnard campuses, and you don't ever hear about people getting in trouble for it."

○ "For Barnard, **freshman housing is completely dry,** drug and smoke free."

○ "I would think that **strictness as far as drinking in the dorms would really depend on which dorm you live in**. It would probably be more difficult to get away with things in the Quad than it would be in one of the apartments Barnard has off campus."

○ "I have no idea how strict the campus police are because **it's not really very hard to follow the rules.** I just have no personal experience."

○ "I have never heard of incident where they enforced a rule on campus, so **I assume it's pretty lax**."

○ "**I sometimes forget that drinking on campus is against the rules** because it's so incredibly common."

Q "Barnard has some **pretty strict policies** but some very lenient enforcement."

Q "Barnard says that they don't allow a lot of things, but you can expect to be warned that **your RA will check your room for contraband** at least three days ahead of time and it will only happen once a semester. It seems like the rules are really just there for show."

The College Prowler Take On...
Campus Strictness

When you get into Barnard, one of the first things you will start to read are all the rules. You will probably worry that you might get in trouble at school for doing something and your parents will be so pleased to see that the college takes such a strong disciplinary stance. However, the moment you step on campus all of those rules will go out the window. In fact, the only rule that is enforced at all by the school is that you must show ID before entering a college residence and even this is often times bent. It's not because Barnard doesn't care about you, but because it has better things to worry about. Strangely, more rules are enforced by other students than by the college. If you smoke in residential buildings, for example, you can expect that someone will complain about the smell.

Kind of like how the security at Barnard is just there for looks, so are the rules they are supposed to enforce. There are also tons of things that you aren't supposed to bring into the dorms, such as alcohol and anything with an open flame, including candles, but don't expect the desk attendant to say anything to you about whatever you might bring to your room. The desk attendants are a little bit stricter in the freshmen dorms, but even they aren't too concerned with what students do in their rooms just as long as it's not hurting or bothering anyone. Out of respect, students usually "hide" contraband, but there's not really any need to.

The College Prowler™ Grade on

Campus Strictness: A-

A high Campus Strictness grade implies an overall lenient atmosphere; police and RAs are fairly tolerant, and the administration's rules are flexible.

Parking

The Lowdown On...
Parking

Approximate Parking Permit Cost

Permits are not sold

Barnard Parking Services

None

Student Parking Lot?

No

Freshman Allowed to Park?

Yes

Parking Permits:

There are no parking permits at Barnard. Student must fend for themselves finding a spot on the street.

Parking Garages Near Campus:

E&B Garage

137 West 108th Street, between Columbus and Amsterdam Avenue

(212) 865-8315

Rates: $8 from 8 a.m. until 6 p.m., $11 from 7 p.m. until 10 a.m., $15 each 24 hour period

Hours: 24 hours a day, 7 days a week

Morningside Garage

3100 Broadway at LaSalle, 124th Street & Broadway

(212) 864-9877

Rates: $7 for the first hour, $7.50 second hour, $11 for up to 6 hours, $16 each 24 hour period

Hours: 24 hours a day, seven days a week

Riverside Church Garage

120th Street, between Riverside & Claremont Avenue

(212) 870-6736

Rates: Weekdays: $10 for 1 hour, $14 for 2 hours, $18 for 4 hours and $22 until 6 p.m., $28 overnight until 7 a.m., weekends: $7 for 1 hour, $9 for 2 hours, Saturday flat rate of $7 from 6 a.m.-6 p.m., $21 after 6 p.m.-12 a.m., Sunday flat rate of $4 from 7 a.m.-6 p.m., $14 after 6 a.m.-12 a.m.

Hours: Weekdays 6 a.m.-12 a.m. and weekends 7 a.m.-12 a.m.

Did You Know?

Best Places to Find a Parking Spot

Try one of the streets south of campus like 113th or 111th. These are far enough away to perhaps have space. Just don't park north of campus, especially if you have a nice car.

Good Luck Getting a Parking Spot Here:

Anywhere near campus

Common Parking Tickets:

At Barnard, you do not deal with ticket prices arranged by the college. You will get tickets issued by the city.

Students Speak Out On...
Parking

{ **"There's virtually no parking, but I don't know of anyone who actually drives, so it doesn't seem to be a big problem."**

Q **"Don't drive a car to school.** You'll be late to classes trying to find parking and then once you do it will be twenty blocks away and you'll just miss your class altogether. I mean, there are places that people are allowed to park near campus, but you'll only be lucky enough to get those like three times a year."

Q "Horrible! **Do not bring a car!** You will be driving around all day looking for parking and the only parking you'll get is a meter that has a one hour time limit, meanwhile your class is an hour and fifteen minutes long. Then, certain days you just can't park on certain streets—it's horrible!"

Q "I don't know because I've never driven around New York City, but **I doubt you'd be able to find parking**."

Q "I don't think anyone on campus drives in the city. **It's just easier and quicker to take a cab**, subway or train and you don't have to worry about your car getting broken into or getting a ticket."

Q "I have no clue. **No one drives to school at all.** Ha! Seriously, I don't know anyone who drives a car up here."

Q "**It's not easy to park** at all—duh."

Q "I can't imagine that anyone would want to bring a car to campus. **It's really hard to find a spot** and there isn't anywhere that doesn't have some sort of restriction. This isn't really just a Barnard problem, though—it's a New York City problem."

The College Prowler Take On...
Parking

There is really nowhere to park on campus or around campus. If you do drive to Barnard, make sure that you have plenty of time to get where you're going because it is not uncommon for a parking spot search to take more than half hour. The school does not issue parking permits, nor does it have a place for anyone to park except instructors and administrators. This isn't because Barnard doesn't care about how students get to school, but because no one, except people who commute from upstate New York or New Jersey, drives in New York City. It's just much easier to walk, or to take some form of public transportation unless money is not an issue at all.

While Barnard's parking scene is almost laughable, a person has to take into consideration the fact that most students live on campus and of those that live off campus, most live in Manhattan; so they most likely do not need to drive to campus either. New York City's public transportation system is very easy and cheap to use, and that is how most New Yorkers get around in this pedestrian friendly city. This may be strange to people from the South or the West coast, where driving is a must for nearly everyone, but in New York driving is a luxury and not a necessity. Barnard really cannot help the street parking situation around campus because that is run by the city, and to somehow allot for on-campus parking for students would just be unnecessary.

The College Prowler™ Grade on
Parking: F

A high grade in this section indicates that parking is both available and affordable, and that parking enforcement isn't overly severe.

Transportation

The Lowdown On...
Transportation

Ways to Get Around Town

On Campus

University shuttle

Walking

Public Transportation

New York Buses

New York Subway

Taxi Cabs

New York Taxi and Limousine Commission (212) 302-8294

Car Rentals

Alamo, local: (212) 857-1255 national: (800) 327-9633, www.alamo.com

Avis, local: (718) 507-3600 national: (800) 831-2847, www.avis.com

Budget, local: (212)807-8700 national: (800) 527-0700, www.budget.com

Dollar, local: (866) 434-2226; national: (800) 800-4000. www. dollar.com

Enterprise, local: (212) 873-7474 national: (800) 736-8222, www.enterprise.com

→

Car Rentals (*Continued...*)

Hertz, local: (212) 486-5925
national: (800) 654-3131,
www.hertz.com

National, local: (212) 875-8360
national: (800) 227-7368,
www.nationalcar.com

Best Ways to Get Around Town

Walking

Subway

Bus

Cab

Ways to Get Out of Town

Airport
John F. Kennedy International

Airport, (718) 656-4520

JFK is approximately forty-five minutes away from Barnard. There is a flat fee of thirty-five dollars to get there by taxi plus tolls and tip.

LaGuardia Airport,
(718) 533-3400

LGA is approximately thirty minutes away from Barnard by Taxi. The fee by taxi is between $25 and $35 and by bus is $2

Newark International Airport,
(201) 961-6000

EWR is around forty minutes away from Barnard and will cost around $50 plus tolls and tip, or around $12 by train.

Airlines Serving NYC:

American Airlines, (800) 433-7300, www.americanairlines.com

Continental, (800) 523-3273, www.continental.com

Delta, (800) 221-1212, www.delta-air.com

Northwest, (800) 225-2525, www.nwa.com

Southwest, (800) 435-9792, www.southwest.com

TWA, (800) 221-2000, www.twa.com

United, (800) 241-6522, www.united.com

US Airways, (800) 428-4322, www.usairways.com

How to Get to the Airport
Long Island Railroad
(718) 217-5477

The Long Island Railroad conveniently leaves from Penn Station at 34th Street on the Red line stop. This will take you up into Long Island.

New Jersey Transit
(201) 762-5100

The train to Newark International Airport also leaves from Penn Station at 34th Street. A ticket is around eleven dollars and takes you right into the airport.

Taxi
(212) 302-8294

A Cab Ride to the Airport
Costs:JFK- $35 plus tolls and
tip

LGA- $20 plus tolls and tip

JFK- $35 plus tolls and tip

EWR- at least $50, negotiate
with the driver

Metro North
(212) 532-4900

New York State's train system
will take you north into the
mainland of New York.

MTA (buses and subway)
(718) 330-1234

The buses and subway leave
from directly in front of Barnard
and no matter how far, the ride
is always two dollars. The M60
bus will take you directly to the
airport.

Students Speak Out On...
Transportation

"I'm from a place where everyone has a car, so it's been really hard for me to adjust. I can't believe I'm living somewhere where riding in a car is a real luxury."

Q "**The subway is right in front of the main entrance** and its just two dollars to go anywhere in Manhattan."

Q "**I've recently fallen in love with the buses.** They're less crowded and more slow paced. Going somewhere on a bus when you're not in a hurry can really let you see the city and it's much cheaper than a cab."

Q "Public transportation in New York is really simple. **The subway system makes it easy to get around** for a reasonable fare, and taxis are always available as well."

Q "It's the city. There are trains and buses available everywhere and all the time. *Depending on when you want to go,* **the subway can be very crowded,** so you should be careful."

Q "**Public transportation is very convenient.** The subway is right next to campus and it will take you almost anywhere in Manhattan in about forty-five minutes or less."

Q "Public transportation is always available, and **it's very easy to use once you learn the names and stops** of the lines that run."

Q "Transportation in New York is like a maze, and sometimes I'm not sure if I'm going the right way until I walk out of the subway station. The subway is just like anything else, though—**practice and you'll get better**."

The College Prowler Take On...
Transportation

You'll be hard pressed to find a city with more convenient transportation than New York City. The subway runs all over Manhattan, the Bronx and Brooklyn for two dollars a ride with free transfers to any other mode of transportation in New York City. There's a subway stop right outside the gates of Barnard that is a part of the one and nine red lines. These subway lines run up and down Broadway in Manhattan, all the way down to South Ferry, making stops at important locations, such as Times Square and Penn Station.

It's very easy to transfer to other subways lines, like the green line, that runs on the east side of Manhattan, or the shuttle train to Grand Central Station from Times Square. Penn Station Houses the Long Island Railroad and the New Jersey Railroad that stops at Newark Airport. Buses around Barnard are also very convenient. In fact, the M60, which also stops in front of the gates will take you directly to New York's La Guardia Airport in less than one hour. This is very helpful for students on a budget, because it can take you and your bags to the airport for two dollars as opposed to thirty or forty dollars in a taxi.

Barnard students are lucky to have access to the variety of transportation that they have available. The only bad thing about it is that most modes of transportation are expensive, especially cabs and trains. Another bad thing is that most ways of getting anywhere, except for in a cab or to LaGuardia on a bus involve transferring to a different mode of transportation at some point, which is both time consuming and expensive. The best thing by far that Barnard has to offer is the M60 bus to the airport and the 116th Subway Station that is less than three minutes from anywhere on campus.

The College Prowler™ Grade on
Transportation: A+

A high grade for Transportation indicates that campus buses, public buses, cabs, and rental cars are readily-available and affordable. Other determining factors include proximity to an airport and the necessity of transportation.

Weather

The Lowdown On...
Weather

Average Temperature		Average Precipitation	
Fall:	57 °F	Fall:	4.15 in.
Winter:	35 °F	Winter:	3.74 in.
Spring:	53 °F	Spring:	4.45 in.
Summer:	74 °F	Summer:	4.23 in.

Students Speak Out On...
Weather

{ **"The weather is cold in the winter and humid in the summer. Bring a heavy coat and lots of sweaters and also summer clothes, because when it's hot, it's hot!"**

Q "Weather comes in extremes—**it is good to bring a variety of clothes**."

Q "Cold, cold winters usually starting in November, sometimes lasting all the way until April. **Bring a good winter coat**, gloves, scarves, sweaters, etc."

Q "People complain that its too cold in the winter and too hot in the summer, but really **the weather is just normal**. Winter is cold and summer is hot, just like it's supposed to be."

Q "The **weather changes all the time**—it's totally unpredictable. Bring a variety of clothes and lots of money—you're going to go shopping."

Q "Come with jeans, t-shirts and sweatshirts, and then you can buy warm coats here. **It gets cold in the winter time**. It was negative during break, but for the most part stays in the twenties or thirties."

Q "Make sure you **bring clothes for all sorts of weather** conditions because it's never the same from one day to the next."

Q "It's so easy to go buy coats in the winter to fix the cold, cold winter, but **summer is miserable** because there's nothing you can do to escape your air-condition-less room."

The College Prowler Take On...
Weather

The good thing about weather in New York is that there are four distinct seasons. In the winter it is very cold—sweaters, long coats, hats, gloves and scarves are a must during this time. Winter also seems to go on forever, so be prepared for those long dreary months and dreading going to class because it's so cold outside. There is a rumor that Columbia did an experiment that proved the intersection of Broadway and 116th Street was the windiest intersection in all of New York City. Spring and fall are the nicest times with the most moderate temperatures, although people from the south and California may still find these seasons a little bit chilly. Summer tends to strike without warning during reading week or finals, which makes sitting inside studying or taking tests next to impossible. Summers in New York are very hot and muggy though, so make sure warm clothes are not the only thing that you bring. You should also bring a fan, since most buildings don't have air conditioning.

New York tends to have decent weather and normally doesn't have temperatures that are too extreme, but the weather is so unpredictable that it is hard to enjoy. You have to change clothes sometimes several times a day to keep up with the changing weather. Also, there are more than a fair share of dreary gray days, which make for a very 'big city' type of atmosphere, but it can get old quickly.

B-

The College Prowler™ Grade on

Weather: B-

A high Weather grade designates that temperatures are mild and rarely reach extremes, that the campus tends to be sunny rather than rainy, and that weather is fairly consistent rather than unpredictable.

Report Card Summary

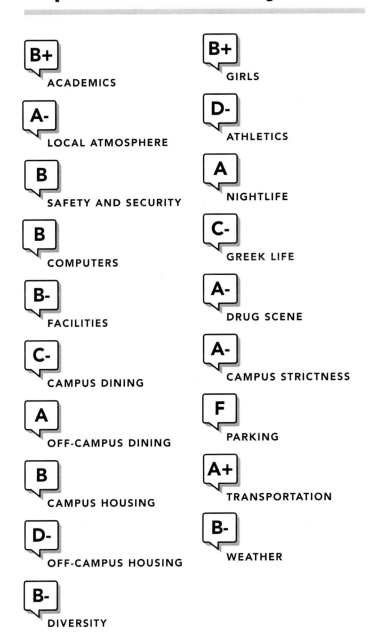

B+ ACADEMICS

A- LOCAL ATMOSPHERE

B SAFETY AND SECURITY

B COMPUTERS

B- FACILITIES

C- CAMPUS DINING

A OFF-CAMPUS DINING

B CAMPUS HOUSING

D- OFF-CAMPUS HOUSING

B- DIVERSITY

B+ GIRLS

D- ATHLETICS

A NIGHTLIFE

C- GREEK LIFE

A- DRUG SCENE

A- CAMPUS STRICTNESS

F PARKING

A+ TRANSPORTATION

B- WEATHER

Overall Experience

Students Speak Out On...
Overall Experience

{ **"Barnard has really opened my eyes to what being a modern woman really is. This school has taught me that I can want it all and have it all."**

Q "I enjoy Barnard a lot! **I wouldn't want to be anywhere else.**"

Q "Barnard is alright, although if I had it to do over **I would like a college with a more "college-y" atmosphere.** The girls at Barnard sometimes act like they're already grown professionals."

Q "I've enjoyed every second at Barnard so far, but **my first year was really tough.** I don't know if I can do three more."

Q "I've had a good experience in the city. **It offers a lot of things that other schools cannot.** Because it's in New York City, but not at the heart of the city, it becomes possible to create a sense of community but still have outside attractions and lots to do."

Q "**I wasn't sure if Barnard was the right choice for me** when I came here, but now I am much more confident of my decision. I've thought about transferring before, but I guess since I haven't made time to do it, I don't really want to."

Q "**I can't imagine being anywhere else**. I'm not even really sure how I ended up here, but now that I'm here, I can't imagine leaving. School gets rough sometimes, but in general, the positive outweighs the negative."

Q "I really like the campus. **It's been a good experience** so far."

Q "Sometimes **I wish I were elsewhere for the social aspect,** but at other times I am so happy I decided to come to Barnard that I can't imagine, nor would I want to be somewhere else."

The College Prowler Take On...
Overall Experience

Barnard College provides a great experience for women who want it all. There is a nice small college feel from small discussion classes and one-on-one advising while being able to take part in a large Ivy League university.

There are large libraries, well equipped athletic facilities and well known faculty at a school where the president of the college might serve you breakfast at midnight before finals.

Most students find that Barnard is a place to feel at home in one of the busiest cities in the world. On the flip side, many students also feel the pressure of tough academic work as well. With so much to do in New York City, and on campus, it can be very frustrating for students when they have to spend hours on homework and studying.

Barnard appears to work very diligently at making sure that it is both academically very rigorous, and that students have many opportunities to enrich their lives socially and financially. This is both a blessing and a curse, because class work takes up such a great deal of time. A few students wish that Barnard had more of a social scene, but most students love the school and continue to feel like they are a part of the community even after they have graduated and moved on.

Barnard is not the school for everyone, but the women that choose it are usually really glad they did. It provides a very unique college experience, much different than the pop culture idea of college that includes rowdy football games and empty kegs lying on the lawns of frat houses.

The Inside Scoop

The Lowdown On...
The Inside Scoop

Barnard Slang

Know the slang, know the school. The following is a list of things you really need to know before coming to Barnard. The more of these words you know, the better off you'll be.

Courseworks- The network Columbia maintains that teachers post grades, homework, and class notes on.

Ebear- The network Barnard students use to sign up for classes and to check grades.

L Courses- These are courses with limited enrollment that you must physically sign up for with the registrar before you are officially in the class. You'll want to get up early to sign up if getting in the class is important to you because L courses fill up fast.

Mac- The McIntosh Student Center is the only student center for Barnard students on campus. This is where Java City, the mailroom, and the College Activities Office are located.

Points- Points are what Barnard calls their credit hours. They look and act like what credit hours are at other schools, but don't expect them to always add up to hours spent in class.

→

Programming- This is what Barnard calls registering for classes.

The Lawn- The Lawn is located in front of Lehman Library.

Registration- This is what you do when you arrive at school to let them know you will actually be attending classes, not when you actually sign up for classes.

Shopping for Classes- Barnard students have a two week window in which they may attend as many classes as they want before they finalize their schedule with their advisor called "shopping"

Things I Wish I Knew Before Coming to Barnard

If you take a class and you don't expect to do as well as you like, it is always better for your GPA to drop the class and take a W rather than to see what you get in the end, because at Barnard you cannot replace poor grades by retaking the class like you can at many other colleges. They will allow you to retake any class you like, but both grades you get for the course will be figured into your overall GPA.

Make sure you really look for interesting classes and good professors during the shopping period at the beginning of the semester, since after this time it is difficult to get out of a bad class.

Tips to Succeed at Barnard

Try to avoid taking more than one course with a lab in a semester. Lab courses tend to demand much more time and effort than other classes, and so taking more than one unless you absolutely must could be detrimental to your other school work.

Get a meal plan with fewer meals and more points. You can use points to buy a meal in the dining hall and to buy coffee and snacks at Java City, but you can only use a meal in the dining hall. You can always get more points if you don't have enough. This will give you more flexibility in where and when you eat.

that often.

Barnard Urban Legends

It is rumored that on Martha Stewart's notes to sell the Imclone stock that got her convicted of insider trading, that there was also a note to send gift money to Barnard College, her alma mater.

School Spirit

Barnard women really love their school. Each year this school spirit really comes out during the "I Love BC" spirit day. Of course, Barnard students love their school year round, but this is really the only time that it comes out. Sometimes it is really hard to identify as a Barnard student when fewer people know Barnard as compared to Columbia, and most students really feel as though they are part of both communities, given that everyone takes classes together and Barnard girls don't have their own athletic teams.

Traditions

"I Love Barnard" Spirit Day- Once a year Barnard hold a spirit day in which the school sells t-shirts, holds a barbeque out on the lawn for all students and gives away all sorts of Barnard goodies. This event really brings students together as a college to appreciate Barnard and what it means to each student.

Greek Games- Each year during the spring, Barnard holds the Greek Games which brings together its students and each class for friendly competition in games such as tug of war.

Midnight Breakfast- This event is held twice a year at the end of reading week, right before finals start and is sponsored by McIntosh Activities Council. Volunteers and administrators, even the college's President, serve food like waffles and eggs to hungry students who are about to take their semester finals.

Big Sub to Traditions: At Big Sub, which is sponsored by McAC and held in the fall, students help build a huge 705 ft. sub sandwich that stretches all over campus. The sandwich is rumored to be totally gone in less than ten minutes.

Finding a Job or Internship

The Lowdown On...
Finding a Job or Internship

The Office of Career Development at Barnard is fantastic. They offer free help writing cover letters and resumes on a daily drop in basis. OCD also offers career counseling for those that aren't sure what they want to do when they graduate. Because Barnard has such a great reputation for educating stellar women, many high profile companies offer internship for either the fall, spring or summer semesters or year round. In the past, internships have been offered at ABC, NBC, MTV, the New York Times, PAPER magazine, the Brooklyn Botanic Garden, the office of Senator Hillary Clinton and Morgan Stanley. There really is a job or internship for everyone including art galleries, sports teams, law firms, brokerage firms or publishing companies. The internships range from no pay up to $15 per hour. The search for an internship is also quite simple. Students receive a username and password and are then able to search for jobs on the internet.

Finding a Job or Internship (*Continued...*)

Another thing career services offers for Barnard students to make money is the Barnard Babysitting Service and the Barnard Bartending Agency. At the Babysitting Service, a student pays five dollars to register and is then able to search for jobs whenever it is convenient. The Bartending Service works nearly the same way except students must take a hundred dollar class to learn bartending skills. These services are very helpful to students because they allow them to connect with people needing a service and to work only when it is convenient.

Advice

The best advice is to be persistent. If you can't find a job that suits your needs at first, just keep looking because new jobs are added every day. If you still can't find what you are looking for, make sure you drop by the Office of Career Development located at 11 Milbank (the basement) where they might be able to help you in your job search. Finally, I would recommend using the Babysitting or Bartending Services to make quick money with a flexible schedule, but use OCD to help you find an internship or job that will really build your resume. The best time to look for these jobs is either at the very beginning of the semester or the end of the semester before you're looking to intern.

Career Center Resources & Services

Cover letter and resume writing help
Online job and internship search

Alumni

The Lowdown On...
Alumni

Website:
http://www.barnard.edu/alum/

Office:
Vagelos Alumnae Center
Located between the Barnard Store and Hewitt on the first floor
3009 Broadway
New York, NY 10027
(212) 854-2005

Services Available

Alumnae Directory- A directory of all former Barnard students that is password protected for security.

Alumnae Message Boards- A place to post messages to other Barnard alums.

Auditing Courses- Barnard alumnae are able to audit many courses that are offered.

Email Forwarding – Barnard Alumnae are given a permanent e-mail address and messages sent to that account may be forwarded to any other email the user specifies.Facility **Use** – Barnard alumnae may be issued an identification card that can be used to gain entrance to the libraries and fitness facilities on campus.

Major Alumnae Events

Alumnae Affairs holds class reunions during May and June each year. Classes have reunions on five year intervals.

Alumnae Publications

Barnard Magazine

The award-winning Barnard magazine is sent quarterly to all alumnae who have a current address on file with Alumnae Records.

Did You Know?

Famous Barnard Alums—

Anna Quindlen (Class of '74) –
Journalist, Pulitzer Prize Winner

Martha Stewart (Class of '63) – Entrepreneur, Convicted Felon

Twyla Tharp (Class of '63) –
Choreographer, Tony and Emmy Award Winner

Jhumpa Lahiri (Class of '89) –
Author, Pulitzer Prize Winner

Joan Rivers (Class of '54) - Entertainer

Margaret Mead (Class of '23) - Anthropologist

Zora Neale Hurston (Class of '28) – Author

Cynthia Nixon (Class of '88) - Actress

Erica Jong (Class of '63) - Author

Student Organizations

Accion Boricua- http://www.columbia.edu/cu/accion

Action for Immigrant Rights

African Students Association- http://www.columbia.edu/cu/asa

Ahimsa- club that centers on the Jain religion. http://www.columbia.edu/cu/ahimsa

American Civil Liberties Union (ACLU)- http://www.columbia.edu/cu/aclu

American Institute of Aeronautics and Astronautics (AIAA)- http://www.columbia.edu/cu/aiaa

American Institute of Chemical Engineers (AIChE)- http://www.columbia.edu/cu/aiche

American Medical Student Association (AMSA)

American Society of Civil Engineers (ASCE)- http://www.seas.columbia.edu/asce

American Society of Mechanical Engineers (ASME) www.asme.org

Amnesty International- http://www.columbia.edu/cu/amnestyinternational/

Anime Club- http://www.columbia.edu/cu/anime

Arab Students' Organization (Turath)- http://www.columbia.edu/cu/turath

Armenian Club- http://www.columbia.edu/cu/armenian

Asian American Alliance (AAA)- http://www.columbia.edu/cu/aaa

Asian American Society of Engineers (AASE)- http://www.columbia.edu/cu/aase/index.html

Asian Baptist Student Koinonia (ABSK)- http://www.columbia.edu/cu/absk/

Association for Computing Machinery (ACM)- http://www.cs.columbia.edu/acm

Athletes in Action

Augustine Club- explores the tradition of Christian Intellectualism- http://www.columbia.edu/cu/augustine/

Bach Society- http://www.bachsociety.com

Baha'i Club- http://www.columbia.edu/cu/bahai

Bhakti Club

Biomedical Engineering Society- http://www.bme.columbia.edu

Black Organization of Soul Sisters (BOSS) – http://www.columbia.edu/cu/boss/

Black Students Organization (BSO) – http://www.columbia.edu/cu/bso/

Black Theater Ensemble – http://www.columbia.edu/cu/bte

Blue and White- http://www.columbia.edu/cu/bw

Blue Key Society- http://www.columbia.edu/cu/bluekey

Brazillian Society

Cantonese Christian Fellowship

Care for Kids

Caribbean Students' Association (CSA)

Chandler Society for Undergrad Chemistry – http://www.columbia.edu/cu/chandler

Charles Drew Premedical Society

Chess Club http://www.columbia.edu/cu/chess

Chicano Caucus http://www.columbia.edu/cu/chicanocaucus

Chinese Student Club (CSC) http://www.columbia.edu/cu/csc

Clefhangers (coed a capella) http://www.columbia.edu/cu/clefs

Club Bangla http://www.columbia.edu/cu/bangla

Club Zamana http://www.columbia.edu/cu/zamana

Columbia Adaptive Sports Organization (CASO) http://www.columbia.edu/cu/caso

Columbia Anti-War Coalition

Columbia Architecture Society

Columbia Atheists and Agnostics

Columbia Biological Society http://www.columbia.edu/cu/bioclub

Columbia Buddhist Meditation Group

Columbia Catholic Athletes http://www.columbia.edu/cu/earl/ccm/cca

Columbia Catholic Undergraduates http://www.columbia.edu/cu/ccm/ccu

Columbia Chinese Bible Study Group http://www.columbia.edu/cu/ccbsg

Columbia College Conservative Club (C4) http://www.columbia.edu/cu/conservative

Columbia College Libertarians http://www.columbia.edu/cu/libertarians

Columbia College Republicans http://www.columbia.edu/cu/cuccr

Columbia College Student Council (CCSC) http://www.columbia.edu/cu/ccsc

Columbia Community Outreach http://www.columbia.edu/cu/outreach

Columbia Concerts http://www.columbia.edu/cu/concerts

Columbia Financial Investment Group http://www.columbia.edu/cu/cfig

Columbia Forum for Society, Science and Religion (CFSSR) http://www.columbia.edu/cu/cssr/cfssr

Columbia Global Justice http://www.columbia.edu/cu/globaljustice

Columbia Greens

Columbia Iranian Students Association http://www.columbia.edu/cu/iran

Columbia Men Against Violence http://www.columbia.edu/cu/cmav

Columbia Military Society

Columbia Music Presents http://www.columbia.edu/cu/cmp

Columbia Musical Theatre Society (CMTS) http://www.columbia.edu/cu/cmts

Columbia Neuroscience Society http://www.columbia.edu/cu/dept/cns

Columbia New Music http://www.columbia.edu/cu/newmusic

Columbia Organization of Rising Entrepreneurs (CORE) http://www.columbia.edu/cu/core

Columbia Political Union http://www.columbia.edu/cu/cpu

Columbia Sign Language Club (was CU Sign) http://www.columbia.edu/cu/soul

Columbia Sikh Student Association

Columbia Student Solidarity Network http://www.columbia.edu/cu/cssn

Columbia Students for Christ http://www.columbia.edu/cu/ccc

Columbia Television (CTV) http://www.columbia.edu/cu/ctv

Columbia Transit Authority (CTA)

Columbia UNICEF

Columbia University Chinese Students and Scholars Association (CUCSSA) http://www.columbia.edu/cu/cucssa

Columbia University College Democratshttp://www.columbiadems.com

Columbia University Film Productions (CUFP) (previously CUPDC) http://www.columbia.edu/cu/cufp

Columbia University Mock Trial http://www.columbia.edu/cu/mocktrial

Columbia University Performing Arts League (CUPAL) http://www.columbia.edu/cu/cupal

Columbia Women's Business Society (CWBS)

Columbia-China Business Association (CCBA) http://www.columbia.edu/cu/ccba

Commission on Elections, Nominations and Appointments (CENA) http://www.columbia.edu/cu/cena

Community Impact http://www.columbia.edu/cu/ci

Conversio Varium (BDSM Informational Group) http://www.columbia.edu/cu/cv

Culinary Society of Columbia University http://www.columbia.edu/cu/culinary

CU Swing http://www.columbia.edu/cu/swing

DC Vote of Barnard-Columbia

Democracy Matters

Dolé

Economics Society http://www.columbia.edu/cu/econsoc

Elementary Hip-Hop http://www.columbia.edu/cu/elementary

Elysium

Everyone Allied Against Homophobia (EAAH) http://www.columbia.edu/cu/eaah

Falun Dafa

Ferris Reel Film Society http://www.columbia.edu/cu/frfs

Friends of the Spartacus Youth Club

French Culture Club http://www.columbia.edu/cu/frenchclub

Games Club http://www.columbia.edu/cu/games

Glee Club http://www.columbia.edu/cu/glee

Golden Key Society http://www.columbia.edu/cu/goldenkey

Gospel Choir http://www.columbia.edu/cu/gospel

Grupo Quisqueyano (GQ) http://www.columbia.edu/cu/gq

Haitian Students' Association (HSA) http://www.columbia.edu/cu/hsa

Hapa Club http://www.columbia.edu/cu/hapa

Hellas http://www.columbia.edu/cu/hellas

Hillel Http://www.hillel.columbia.edu

Hindu Students Organization http://www.columbia.edu/cu/hso

Hong Kong Students and Scholars Society http://www.columbia.edu/cu/hksss

Human Rights Society

Iberia: Spanish Association at Columbia http://www.columbia.edu/cu/iberia

International Socialist Organization (ISO) http://www.columbia.edu/cu/bbb/polit/moreinfo/inter

InterVarsity Christian Fellowship http://www.columbia.edu/cu/ivcf

Japan Club http://www.columbia.edu/cu/japanclub

Jazz Band http://www.columbia.edu/cu/bbb/moreinfo/jazz/band

Jubilation! (coed a capella) www.jube.com

Karaoke Club

Kings Crown Shakespeare Troupe http://www.columbia.edu/cu/shakespeare

Kingsmen (a capella) http://www.columbia.edu/cu/kingsmen

Korea Campus Crusade for Christ http://www.columbia.edu/cu/kccc

Korean Christian Students Association

Korean Students Association (KSA) www.columbiaksa.org

Latter Day Saints Association (LDSSA)

Liga Fillipina http://www.columbia.edu/cu/liga

Metrotones http://www.columbia.edu/cu/metrotones

Model Congress http://www.columbia.edu/cu/modelcongress

Model European Union Club (MEU) http://www.columbia.edu/cu/bbb/speech/moreinfo/model

Model United Nations (MUN) http://www.columbia.edu/cu/mun

Museo http://www.columbia.edu/cu/museo/6

Museum Club http://www.columbia.edu/cu/museum

Muslim Students Association http://www.columbia.edu/cu/msa

National Society of Black Engineers (NSBE) http://www.columbia.edu/cu/nsbe

Native American Council http://www.columbia.edu/cu/nahc

Nightline (Peer Counseling) http://www.columbia.edu/cu/nightline

Non Sequitur (a capella) http://www.columbia.edu/cu/nonsequitur

Notes and Keys (coed a capella) http://www.columbia.edu/cu/bbb/perf/moreinfo/notes

Opera Ensemble http://www.columbia.edu/cu/opera

Orchesis (Dance) http://www.columbia.edu/cu/orchesis

Organization of Pakistani Students (OPS) http://www.columbia.edu/cu/ops

Orthodox Christian Fellowship http://www.columbia.edu/cu/ocf

Parliamentary Debate Team http://www.columbia.edu/cu/debate

Peace Collective

Philolexian Society http://www.columbia.edu/cu/philo

Policy Debate Team http://www.columbia.edu/cu/pdt

Political Science Student Association (PSSA) http://www.columbia.edu/cu/pssa

Postscrypt Art Gallery http://www.columbia.edu/cu/postcrypt/artgallery

Postcrypt Coffeehouse http://www.columbia.edu/cu/postcrypt/coffeehouse

Prangstgrup www.prangstgrup.com

Productive Outreach for Women

Project Success

Queer Alliance http://www.columbia.edu/cu/lbgc

Queers of Color http://www.columbia.edu/cu/qoc

Quiz Bowl http://www.columbia.edu/cu/cbowl

Raw Elementz http://www.columbia.edu/cu/rawelementz

Romanian Society http://www.columbia.edu/cu/romanian

Russian International Association http://www.columbia.edu/cu/ria

Science Fiction Society (CUSFS) http://www.columbia.edu/cu/cusfs

Scientists and Engineers for a Better Society http://www.columbia.edu/

cu/sebs

Seventh Day Adventist Students Society

Singapore Students Association http://www.columbia.edu/cu/ssa

Sirens

Six Milks http://www.columbia.edu/cu/sixmilks

Societa Italiana http://www.columbia.edu/cu/societa

Society for International Undergraduates http://www.columbia.edu/cu/international

Society of Automotive Engineering (SAE) http://www.columbia.edu/cu/sae

Society of Hispanic Professional Engineers (SHPE) http://www.columbia.edu/cu/shpe

Society of Women Engineers (SWE) http://www.columbia.edu/cu/bbb/prepro/moreinfo/swomen

Sounds of China http://www.columbia.edu/cu/soc

Student Organization of Latinos (SOL) http://www.columbia.edu/cu/sol

Student Union and Caucuses

Students for Better Global Governance

Students for Choice (SFC) http://www.columbia.edu/cu/sfc

Students for Environmental and Economic Justice (SEEJ)

Students for Sensible Drug Policy (SSDP) http://www.columbia.edu/cu/ssdp

Students Promoting Empowerment and Knowledge (SPEaK) http://www.columbia.edu/cu/speak

Students United for America http://www.columbia.edu/cu/su4a

Taal

Taiwanese American Students Association http://www.columbia.edu/cu/tasa

Thai Sa-Bai http://www.columbia.edu/cu/thai

Tibetan Studies Society

Toward Reconciliation http://www.columbia.edu/cu/tu/home

Turkish Students Association http://www.columbia.edu/cu/tsa

Two Left Feet http://www.columbia.edu/cu/twoleftfeet

Ukranian Students Society http://www.columbia.edu/cu/ukrainian

United Students of Color Council (USCC) http://www.columbia.edu/cu/uscc

University Bible Fellowship http://www.columbia.edu/cu/ubf

Undergraduate Mathematics Society http://www.math.columbia.edu/ums

Undergraduate Housing Council http://www.columbia.edu/cu/uhc

Upstart

Uptown Vocals (coed a capella) http://www.columbia.edu/cu/uptown

Wind Ensemble http://www.columbia.edu/cu/wind

The Best & The Worst

The Ten **BEST** Things About Barnard:

1	Columbia University affiliation
2	The Lawn
3	Midnight Breakfast
4	Doris in the College Activities Office
5	Street Vendors
6	Subways
7	Tom's Diner
8	The tunnel system
9	The Manhattan skyline
10	Alumnae

The Ten WORST Things About Barnard:

1 No air-conditioning in most dorms

2 No retaking classes you've done poorly in

3 The cold, cold winters

4 Only one dining hall open for dinner

5 Loud fraternity guys that live behind the dorms

6 No entrances on the south side of campus

7 The Varsity Sports

8 No Parking

9 Computer lab waits

10 Poor cell phone reception

Visiting Barnard

The Lowdown On...
Visiting Barnard

Hotel Information

Upper West Side:
(less than 10 minutes from campus)

Country Inn Bed & Breakfast
270 West 77th Street
(212) 580-4183
Rates: $150-$200

Hotel Belleclaire
250 West 77th Street (at Broadway)
(212) 362-7700/(877) 468-3522
Rates: $209-$250

Hotel Beacon
2130 Broadway at 75th Street
(212) 787-1100
Rates: $170-$310

Lucerne Hotel
201 West 79th Street
(212) 875-1000
Rates: $180-$340
Parking Available

Milburn Hotel
242 West 76th Street
(212) 362-1006
Rates: $129-$205

➜

Mayflower Hotel

15 Central Park West
(212) 265-0060/(800) 223-4164
Rates: $200+

Riverside Tower Hotel

80 Riverside Drive
(212) 877-5200/800-724-3136
Rates: $84-$120

Radisson Empire Hotel

444 West 63rd Street (Lincoln
Center)
(212) 265-7400/(800) 333-3333
Rates: $160-$250
*Mention Columbia University
Rate

Midtown:

(Between 10 and 15 minutes from campus)

Helmsley Windsor

100 West 58th Street (at 6th
Avenue)
(212) 265-2100/(800) 221-4982
Rates: $165-$215

Holiday Crowne Plaza

1605 West 49th Street (at
Broadway)
(212) 977-4000/(800) 465-4329
Rates: $180-$250

New York Hilton & Tower

1335 6th Avenue (bet
53rd&54th Sts)
(212) 586-7000/(800) 445-8667
Rates: $180-$250

New York Marriott Marquis

1535 West 45th Street (at
Broadway)
(212) 398-1900 /(800) 228-9290
Rates: $180-$250

Novotel New York

226 West 52nd Street (Corner
of B_way)
(212) 315-0100/(800) 221-3185
Rates: $165-$215
*Mention: "Government
Related Rate" (Columbia)

Upper East Side:

(all are at least 15 minutes from campus)

Drake Swiss

440 Park Avenue at 56th Street
(888) 737-9477
Rates: $289
www.candlewoodsuites.com

Franklin

87th & Lexington
(877) 847-4444
Rates: $235

Hotel Wales

1295 Madison Avenue
(877) 847-4444
Rates: $265

Take a Campus Virtual Tour

http://www.barnard.edu/tour/

To Schedule a Group Information Session or Interview:

Call (212) 854-2014 between 9 a.m. and 4:30 p.m.

Interviews are conducted throughout the summer and fall. Saturday interviews are only held during the fall.

Campus Tours

Tours are given daily Monday through Friday at 11:30 a.m. and 3:30 p.m. and do not require an appointment. Tours will not be given during college holidays and breaks. It is recommended that you call in advance to ensure that there will be a tour on the day you are interested in. Campus Tours begin at the Office of Admissions located on the first floor of Milbank Hall.

Overnight Visits:

Overnight visits are only offered for high school seniors and only during the fall semester. Call the Office of Admissions to see if there are any opportunities for an overnight visit.

Directions to Campus

Driving from the North

•New York Thruway (Route 87) or New England Thruway (I-95) to the Cross Bronx Expressway toward the George Washington Bridge. Bear right as you approach the bridge and take the exit for Henry Hudson Parkway South.

•Take the 96th Street exit of the Henry Hudson Parkway (West Side Highway). Go two blocks east to Broadway, and take a left turn uptown to Barnard's main gate at 117th Street.

Driving from the South

•New Jersey Turnpike (I-95) north or 1-80 east to the George Washington Bridge. Exit the bridge onto the Henry Hudson Parkway South.

•Take the 96th Street exit of the Henry Hudson Parkway (West Side Highway). Go two blocks east to Broadway, and take a left turn uptown to Barnard's main gate at 117th Street.

Driving from the East

•Grand Central Parkway or Long Island Expressway west to the Cross Island Parkway north. Cross over the Throgs Neck Bridge to the Cross Bronx Expressway toward the George Washington Bridge. Exit onto the Henry Hudson Parkway South.

•Take the 96th Street exit of the Henry Hudson Parkway (West Side Highway). Go two blocks east to Broadway, and take a left turn uptown to Barnard's main gate at 117th Street.

Driving from the West

•New Jersey Turnpike (I-95) north or 1-80 east to the George Washington Bridge. Exit the bridge onto the Henry Hudson Parkway South.

•Take the 96th Street exit of the Henry Hudson Parkway (West Side Highway). Go two blocks east to Broadway, and take a left turn uptown to Barnard's main gate at 117th Street.

Words to Know

Academic Probation – A student can receive this if they fail to keep up with their school's academic minimums. Those who are unable to improve their grades after receiving this warning can possibly face dismissal.

Beer Pong / Beirut – A drinking game with numerous cups of beer arranged in a particular pattern on each side of a table. The goal is to get a ping pong ball into one of the opponent's cups by throwing the ball or hitting it with a paddle. If the ball lands in a cup, the opponent is required to drink the beer.

Bid – An invitation from a fraternity or sorority to pledge their specific house.

Blue-Light Phone – Brightly-colored phone posts with a blue light bulb on top. These phones exist for security purposes and are located at various outside locations around most campuses. If a student has an emergency or is feeling endangered, they can pick up one of these phones (free of charge) to connect with campus police or an escort service.

Campus Police – Policemen who are specifically assigned to a given institution. Campus police are not regular city officers; they are employed by the university in a full-time capacity.

Club Sports – A level of sports that falls somewhere between varsity and intramural. If a student is unable to commit to a varsity team but has a lot of passion for athletics, a club sport could be a better, less intense option. If a club sport still requires too much commitment, intramurals often involve no traveling and a lot less time.

Cocaine – An illegal drug. Also known as "coke" or "blow," cocaine often resembles a white crystalline or powdery substance. It is highly addictive and dangerous.

Common Application – An application that students can use to apply to multiple schools.

Course Registration – The time when a student selects what courses they would like for the upcoming quarter or semester. Prior to registration, it is best to have an idea of several back-up courses in case a particular class becomes full. If a course is full, a student can place themselves on the waitlist, although this still does not guarantee entry.

Division Athletics – Athletics range from Division I to Division III. Division IA is the most competitive, while Division III is considered to be the least competitive.

Dorm – Short for dormitory, a dorm is an on-campus housing facility. Dorms can provide a range of options from suite-style rooms to more communal options that include shared bathrooms. Most first-year students live in dorms. Some upperclassmen who wish to stay on campus also choose this option.

Early Action – A way to apply to a school and get an early acceptance response without a binding commitment. This is a system that is becoming less and less available.

Early Decision – An option that students should use only if they are positive that a place is their dream school. If a student applies to a school using the early decision option and is admitted, they are required and bound to attend that university. Admission rates are usually higher with early decision students because the school knows that a student is making them their first choice.

Ecstasy – An illegal drug. Also known as "E" or "X," ecstasy looks like a pill and most resembles an aspirin. Considered a party drug, ecstasy is very dangerous and can be deadly.

Ethernet – An extremely fast internet connection that is usually available in most university-owned residence halls. To use an Ethernet connection properly, a student will need a network card and cable for their computer.

Fake ID – A counterfeit identification card that contains false information. Most commonly, students get fake IDs and change their birthdates so that they appear to be older than 21 (of legal drinking age). Even though it is illegal, many college students have fake IDs in hopes of purchasing alcohol or getting into bars.

Frosh – Slang for "freshmen."

Hazing – Initiation rituals that must be completed for membership into some fraternities or sororities. Numerous universities have outlawed hazing due to its degrading or dangerous requirements.

Sports (IMs) – A popular, and usually free, student activity where students create teams and compete against other groups for fun. These sports vary in competitiveness and can include a range of activities—everything from billiards to water polo. IM sports are a great way to meet people with similar interests.

Keg – Officially called a half barrel, a keg contains roughly 200 12-ounce servings of beer and is often found at college parties.

LSD – An illegal drug. Also known as acid, this hallucinogenic drug most commonly resembles a tab of paper.

Marijuana – An illegal drug. Also known as weed or pot; besides alcohol, marijuana is one of the most commonly-found drugs on campuses across the country.

Major –The focal point of a student's college studies; a specific topic that is studied for a degree. Examples of majors include physics, English, history, computer science, economics, business, and music. Many students decide on a specific major before arriving on campus, while others are simply "undecided" and figure it out later. Those who are extremely interested in two areas can also choose to double major.

Meal Block – The equivalent of one meal. Students on a "meal plan" usually receive a fixed number of meals per week.

Each meal, or "block," can be redeemed at the school's dining facilities in place of cash. More often than not, if a student fails to use their weekly allotment of meal blocks, they will be forfeited.

Minor – An additional focal point in a student's education. Often serving as a compliment or addition to a student's main area of focus, a minor has fewer requirements and prerequisites to fulfill than a major. Minors are not required for graduation from most schools; however some students who want to further explore many different interests choose to have both a major and a minor.

Mushrooms – An illegal drug. Also known as "shrooms," this drug looks like regular mushrooms but are extremely hallucinogenic.

Off-Campus Housing – Housing from a particular landlord or rental group that is not affiliated with the university. Depending on the college, off-campus housing can range from extremely popular to non-existent. Those students who choose to live off campus are typically given more freedom, but they also have to deal with things such as possible subletting scenarios, furniture, and bills. In addition to these factors, rental prices and distance often affect a student's decision to move off campus.

Office Hours – Time that teachers set aside for students who have questions about the coursework. Office hours are a good place for students to go over any problems and to show interest in the subject material.

Pledging – The time after a student has gone through rush, received a bid, and has chosen a particular fraternity or sorority they would like to join. Pledging usually lasts anywhere from one to two semesters. Once the pledging period is complete and a particular student has done everything that is required to become a member, they are considered a brother or sister. If a fraternity or a sorority would decide to "haze" a group of students, these initiation rituals would take place during the pledging period.

Private Institution – A school that does not use taxpayers dollars to help subsidize education costs. Private schools typically cost more than public schools and are usually smaller.

Prof – Slang for "professor."

Public Institution – A school that uses taxpayers dollars to help subsidize education costs. Public schools are often a good value for in-state residents and tend to be larger than most private colleges.

Quarter System (sometimes referred to as the Trimester System) – A type of academic calendar system. In this setup, students take classes for three academic periods. The first quarter usually starts in late September or early October and concludes right before Christmas. The second quarter usually starts around early to mid–January and finishes up around March or April. The last quarter, or "third quarter," usually starts in late March or early April and finishes up in late May or Mid-June. The fourth quarter is summer. The major difference between the quarter system and semester system is that students take more courses but with less coverage.

RA (Resident Assistant) – A student leader who is assigned to a particular floor in a dormitory in order to help to the other students who live there. A RA's duties include ensuring student safety and providing guidance or assistance wherever possible.

Recitation – An extension of a specific course; a "review" session of sorts. Because some classes are so large, recitations offer a setting with fewer students where students can ask questions and get help from professors or TAs in a more personalized environment. As a result, it is common for most large lecture classes to be supplemented with recitations.

Rolling Admissions – A form of admissions. Most commonly found at public institutions, schools with this type of policy continue to accept students throughout the year until their class sizes are met. For example, some schools begin accepting students as early as December and will continue to do so until April or May.

Room and Board – This is typically the combined cost of a university-owned room and a meal plan.

Room Draw/Housing Lottery – A common way to pick on-campus room assignments for the following year. If a student decides to remain in university-owned housing, they are assigned a unique number that, along with seniority, is used to choose their new rooms for the next year.

Rush – The period in which students can meet the brothers and sisters of a particular chapter and find out if a given fraternity or sorority is right for them. Rushing a fraternity or a sorority is not a requirement at any school. The goal of rush is to give students who are serious about pledging a feel for what to expect.

Semester System – The most common type of academic calendar system at college campuses. This setup typically includes two semesters in a given school year. The "fall" semester starts around the end of August or early September and finishes right before winter vacation. The "spring" semester usually starts in mid-January and ends around late April or May.

Student Center/Rec Center/Student Union – A common area on campus that often contains study areas, recreation facilities, and eateries. This building is often a good place to meet up with fellow students and is most commonly used as a hangout. Depending on the school, the student center can have a huge role or a non-existent role in campus life.

Student ID – A university-issued photo ID that serves as a student's key to many different functions within an institution. Some schools require students to show these cards in order to get into dorms, libraries, cafeterias, and other facilities. In addition to storing meal plan information, in some cases, a student ID can actually work as a debit card and allow students to purchase things from bookstores or local shops.

Suite – A type of dorm room. Unlike other places that have communal bathrooms that are shared by the entire floor, a suite has a private bathroom. Suite-style dorm rooms can house anywhere from two to ten students.

TA (Teacher's Assistant) – An undergraduate or grad student who helps in some manner with a specific course. In some cases, a TA will teach a class, assist a professor, grade assignments, or conduct office hours.

Undergraduate – A student who is in the process of studying for their Bachelor (college) degree.

ABOUT THE AUTHOR:

I still cannot believe how much there is to know about Barnard College, and how much I've learned since transferring in. Writing this book really opened my eyes to both the good and the bad of Barnard, and has taught me some things about being aware of my surroundings.

I am a junior Psychology major who isn't quite sure what her plans are after college. Hopefully, the future will include furthering my education in graduate school somewhere closer to my home in Ft. Worth, Texas. New York has been a great experience for me so far, and I sincerely hope that you feel like you've gotten to know Barnard a little bit better. Good luck to anyone reading this in finding your future home away from home at college.

I would like to extend a very special thanks to those a CollegeProwler who gave me this awesome opportunity, my brother who graciously let me use the computer compulsively, Memaw and Papa for their support in all of my crazy endeavors, my mom and dad who gave me the skills and opportunity to attend college at all, and finally to my best friend and future, Eddie.

Megan Cloud, Author
Barnard College

megancloud@collegeprowler.com

Notes

....
....
....
....
....
....
....
....
....
....
....
....
....

Notes

Notes

....

....

....

....

....

....

....

....

....

....

....

....

....

Notes

....

....

....

....

....

....

....

....

....

....

....

....

....

Notes

···

···

···

···

···

···

···

···

···

···

···

···

···

···

Notes

....

....

....

....

....

....

....

....

....

....

....

....

....

Notes

....

....

....

....

....

....

....

....

....

....

....

....

....

Notes

....

....

....

....

....

....

....

....

....

....

....

....

....

Notes

....

....

....

....

....

....

....

....

....

....

....

....

....

Notes

Notes

....

....

....

....

....

....

....

....

....

....

....

....

....

Notes

Notes

....
....
....
....
....
....
....
....
....
....
....
....
....
....

Notes

....

....

....

....

....

....

....

....

....

....

....

....

....

Notes

Notes

....

....

....

....

....

....

....

....

....

....

....

....

....

Notes

....

....

....

....

....

....

....

....

....

....

....

....

....

Notes

....

....

....

....

....

....

....

....

....

....

....

....

....

Need More Help?

Do you have more questions about this school? Can't find a certain statistic? College Prowler is here to help. We are the best source of college information on the planet. We have a network of thousands of students who can get the latest information on any school to you ASAP. E-mail us at *info@collegeprowler.com* with your college-related questions. It's like having an older sibling show you the ropes!

Email Us Your College-Related Questions!

Check out **www.collegeprowler.com** for more details.
1.800.290.2682

Notes

....

....

....

....

....

....

....

....

....

....

....

....

Tell Us What Life Is Really Like At Your School!

Have you ever wanted to let people know what your school is really like? Now's your chance to help millions of high school students choose the right school.

Let your voice be heard and win cash and prizes!

Check out **www.collegeprowler.com** for more info!

Notes

....

....

....

....

....

....

....

....

....

....

....

....

....

Do You Have What It Takes To Get Admitted?

The College Prowler Road to College Counseling Program is here. An admissions officer will review your candidacy at the school of your choice and create a 12+ page personal admission plan. We rate your credentials with the same criteria used by school admissions committees. We assess your strengths and weaknesses and create a plan of action that makes a difference.

Check out **www.collegeprowler.com** or call 1.800.290.2682 for complete details.

Notes

....

....

....

....

....

....

....

....

....

....

....

....

....

Pros and Cons

Still can't figure out if this is the right school for you?
You've already read through this in-depth guide; why not
list the pros and cons? It will really help with narrowing down
your decision and determining whether or not
this school is right for you.

Pros	Cons

Notes

....

....

....

....

....

....

....

....

....

....

....

....

....

Need Help Paying For School?

Apply for our Scholarship!

College Prowler awards thousands of dollars a year
to students who compose the best essays.
E-mail *scholarship@collegeprowler.com* for more
information, or call 1.800.290.2682.

Apply now at **www.collegeprowler.com**

Notes

Get Paid To Rep Your City!

Make money for college!

Earn cash by telling your friends about College Prowler!

Excellent Pay + Incentives + Bonuses

Compete with reps across the nation for cash bonuses

Gain marketing and communication skills

Build your resume and gain work experience for future career opportunities

Flexible work hours; make your own schedule

Opportunities for advancement

Contact *sales@collegeprowler.com*
Apply now at **www.collegeprowler.com**

Notes

....

....

....

....

....

....

....

....

....

....

....

....

....

Do You Own A Website?

Would you like to be an affiliate of one of the fastest-growing companies in the publishing industry? Our web affiliates generate a significant income based on customers whom they refer to our website. Start making some cash now! Contact *sales@collegeprowler.com* for more information or call 1.800.290.2682

Apply now at **www.collegeprowler.com**

Notes

....

....

....

....

....

....

....

....

....

....

....

....

Reach A Market Of Over 24 Million People.

Advertising with College Prowler will provide you with an environment in which your message will be read and respected. Place your message in a College Prowler guidebook, and let us start bringing long-lasting customers to you. We deliver high-quality ads in color or black-and-white throughout our guidebooks.

Contact Joey Rahimi
joey@collegeprowler.com
412.697.1391
1.800.290.2682

Check out **www.collegeprowler.com** for more info.

Notes

....

....

....

....

....

....

....

....

....

....

....

....

....

Write For Us!

Get Published! Voice Your Opinion.

Writing a College Prowler guidebook is both fun and rewarding; our open-ended format allows your own creativity free reign. Our writers have been featured in national newspapers and have seen their names in bookstores across the country. Now is your chance to break into the publishing industry with one of the country's fastest-growing publishers!

Apply now at **www.collegeprowler.com**

Contact *editor@collegeprowler.com* or call 1.800.290.2682 for more details.

Notes

....

....

....

....

....

....

....

....

....

....

....

....

....

Do You Own
A Website?

Would you like to be an affiliate of one of the
fastest-growing companies in the publishing industry?
Our web affiliates generate a significant income
based on customers whom they refer to our
website. Start making some cash now! Contact
sales@collegeprowler.com for more information
or call 1.800.290.2682

Apply now at **www.collegeprowler.com**

Notes

....

....

....

....

....

....

....

....

....

....

....

....

....

Reach A Market Of Over 24 Million People.

Advertising with College Prowler will provide you with an environment in which your message will be read and respected. Place your message in a College Prowler guidebook, and let us start bringing long-lasting customers to you. We deliver high-quality ads in color or black-and-white throughout our guidebooks.

Contact Joey Rahimi
joey@collegeprowler.com
412.697.1391
1.800.290.2682

Check out **www.collegeprowler.com** for more info.

COLLEGE PROWLER™

Notes

....

....

....

....

....

....

....

....

....

....

....

....

....

Write For Us!

Get Published! Voice Your Opinion.

Writing a College Prowler guidebook is both fun and rewarding; our open-ended format allows your own creativity free reign. Our writers have been featured in national newspapers and have seen their names in bookstores across the country. Now is your chance to break into the publishing industry with one of the country's fastest-growing publishers!

Apply now at **www.collegeprowler.com**

Contact *editor@collegeprowler.com* or call 1.800.290.2682 for more details.

Notes

....

....

....

....

....

....

....

....

....

....

....

....